REFUGEE WOMEN

SECOND EDITION

Susan Forbes Martin

LEXINGTON BOOKS

Lanham • Boulder • New York • Toronto • Oxford

LEXINGTON BOOKS

Published in the United States of America
by Lexington Books
An imprint of The Rowman & Littlefield Publishing Group, Inc.
4501 Forbes Boulevard, Suite 200, Lanham, Maryland 20706

PO Box 317
Oxford
OX2 9RU, UK

British Library Cataloguing in Publication Information Available

Library of Congress Cataloging-in-Publication Data
Martin, Susan Forbes.
    Refugee women / Susan Forbes Martin. — 2nd ed.
        p. cm.
    Includes bibliographical references and index.
    ISBN 0-7391-0753-4 (cloth : alk. paper) — ISBN 0-7391-0589-2 (pbk. : alk. paper)
    1. Women refugees. I. Title.

    HV640.M34 2003
    362.87'082—dc20   2003017755

Printed in the United States of America

Contents

Foreword

In most refugee populations, more than 50 percent of the uprooted people are women and girls. Stripped of the protection of their homes, their government, and often their family structure, females are made particularly vulnerable. They face the rigors of long journeys into exile, official harassment or indifference, and frequent sexual abuse even after reaching an apparent place of safety. Women must cope with these threats while being nurse, teacher, breadwinner, and physical protector of their families.

In the past decade, the UN High Commissioner for Refugees (UNHCR) has worked hard to ensure that women have equal access to protection, basic goods and services as they attempt to rebuild their lives. A commitment to gender equality mainstreaming, coupled with recognition of the special needs of refugee women, has increased efforts to provide better health care, improve food and water supplies, increase literacy and skills training, programs to study and combat sexual violence, and the curse of sexual genital mutilation. Other initiatives have helped women begin their own small businesses and become actively involved in refugee camp committees or other political, social, and economic groups once they returned home.

In spring 2001, I met with fifty refugee women who shared their experiences, offered testimonies, and commented on the response offered by UNHCR and other partners to their concerns. This initiative led to five specific commitments by UNHCR: (1) to ensure that women participate in all refugee management and leadership committees in urban, rural, and camp settings, including in return areas; (2) to register male and female refugees individually and provide individual documentation; (3) to develop integrated country-level strategies to prevent and respond to sexual and gender-based violence; (4) to promote direct participation of refugee women in both food and nonfood management and distribution; and (5) to provide sanitary materials to all women and girls as standard UNHCR assistance practice.

While we have made progress in each of these areas, the work is far from finished. As this book documents, refugee and displaced women still face enormous threats to their safety and security. Far too many refugee women and their families are left without solutions to their displacement. The international community and UNHCR have developed a wealth of international norms, policies, and guidelines to improve the protection and care of refugee women and refugee children. In practice, however, there is still a gap in the application and implementation of these, owing to resource constraints (both financial and human), uneven priorities and accountability, and the scourge of conflict and repression.

Protection work today demands new tools, new multilateral commitments to ensure burden sharing and durable solutions, new strategies, new thinking, and new partnerships. This book offers many practical recommendations to ensure women's participation, safety, legal protection, and access to humanitarian assistance. By focusing on both refugee and internally displaced women, it recognizes that some of the most vulnerable women are trapped within their own countries. This book importantly focuses on solutions to the crisis of displacement, spelling out ways that women can be resources for the development of their home countries, countries of asylum, and resettlement countries.

Women are the life-sustaining force of any refugee community. We must ensure that their voice is heard, that their potential is developed, and that their role is fully recognized. In introducing the first edition of this book, my predecessor committed "to supporting the efforts of refugee women as partners in finding durable solutions to their situation." It is my pleasure—indeed, obligation—to repeat this commitment as we seek ways to better the lives of the millions who have been displaced throughout the world. This book makes an important contribution to this effort.

Ruud Lubbers
UN High Commissioner for Refugees

Preface

This book outlines the situation of refugee and displaced women, discussing both their needs and the resources that they have to offer. It also describes steps that have been taken by the United Nations, governments, and non-governmental organizations (NGOs) to address their needs and build on their resources. Throughout it makes recommendations for further action to increase protection and assistance for these forced migrants.

This is a fully revised and updated version of a book published in 1992. The original book was intended to raise awareness of the situation of refugee and displaced women throughout the world and to increase knowledge of the ways in which the needs of refugee and displaced women can be more effectively addressed and their contributions can be tapped. It is also intended to encourage discussion and networking on what can be done by organizations involved in humanitarian assistance and development to inform, organize, and work to improve people's understanding of these issues, and to develop programs, campaigns, and strategies which genuinely respond to the needs outlined. Much has changed in the past decade. There is greatly increased awareness that a large majority of forced migrants, particularly in developing countries, are women and their dependent children. Since the publication of *Refugee Women*, the UN High Commissioner for Refugees has promulgated *Guidelines on the Protection of Refugee Women,* as well as more specific guidance in addressing sexual and gender-based violence targeted at refugee women and children. The United Nations has also promoted *Guiding Principles on Internal Displacement*, which emphasizes the special vulnerabilities as well as strengths of women who have been displaced within their own countries.

Despite the increased awareness and understanding of the challenges presented by a largely female and young population, major problems remain in protecting and assisting refugee and displaced women. There are still far too many situations in which women and children are subject to sexual violence and targeted attacks during flight and in refugee and displaced persons camps. Women still find it difficult to feed themselves and their families, and sexual exploitation by armed forces, government officials, and even humanitarian aid workers continues to prevail in too many countries. Access to maternal and child health and reproductive health services has improved tremendously, but these programs are still too few in numbers to meet the total need. Women who are persecuted because of their gender and social roles still find too many barriers to asylum in too many countries. Return to their home communities and resettlement in other countries remain too elusive solutions for too many refugee and displaced women and their children.

This book can be used as a tool to help individuals and groups to stimulate reflective discussion and further research and study, and to encourage creative analysis with regard to possible solutions. It can serve as a basic guide to the subject; as a structure for study and a framework for subsequent action; as a basis for discussion groups and for conferences, workshops, and seminars; and as a means of informing and sensitizing voluntary organizations and government agencies. The audience intended for the book includes local and regional NGOs in both industrialized and developing countries; women's and youth organizations, religious groups, development NGOs, trade unions, and educational establishments; and agencies and programs of the United Nations system. It is also intended for academic audiences, including courses on refugee and humanitarian emergencies, asylum law and policy, development, international relations, conflict management, and others.

The situation of refugee and displaced women and children is discussed in six chapters touching on the following issues:

- the role of refugee and internally displaced women in their communities and their participation in decision making and programming;
- legal and physical protection issues affecting refugee and internally displaced women;
- assistance issues, including access to food, shelter and water, health care, education, and social services;
- economic activities of refugee and displaced women;
- durable solutions in developing countries, including repatriation and permanent settlement in countries of asylum; and
- resettlement in industrialized countries.

The final chapter traces the evolution of policy and programmatic actions at the international level to improve assistance and protection efforts for refugee and displaced women.

My thanks go to two research assistants, Kari Jorgensen and Katherine Stone, who helped me collect information for this book. Kari's help in putting together the tables and bibliography and checking last-minute facts and figures is particularly appreciated. I also benefited from the research activities of the Women's Commission for Refugee Women and Children, and particularly the study directed by my colleague, Patricia Weiss-Fagen, on implementation of the *Guidelines on the Protection of Refugee Women*. My final thanks go to the many refugee and displaced women who have spent hours telling me of their dreams and their needs. It is their story that I have tried to tell in this volume.

Displaced Burundian Women. (Susan Martin)

1

Setting the Stage

We enter the refugee camp through a military guard post. We see rows upon rows of huts, stretching back into the camp for what must be miles. Ringing the huts are larger buildings, housing an infirmary, administration building, rudimentary hospital, training facility, and food warehouse. Off to one side is a school.

Out of the jeep and wandering on foot, our senses are assailed. The smells of cooking food mingle with the stench of latrines. Dress ranges from the most traditional to the most modern, running shoes vying with native costume. Little stalls sell spices, salt, cigarettes, and candy for the children.

One impression stands out above all others, though: The faces of the refugees are overwhelmingly the faces of women and children. For these women, life is hard and often dangerous. They are the victims of war and repression. Many barely survived their flight from Cambodia. Some have been displaced for a decade, watching as children are born far from their homes and grow up amid barbed wire.[1]

About 13 million people are refugees, having been uprooted from their homes and forced to seek safety in other countries (see table 1.1). Another 25–30 million people would be refugees if they crossed an international border but they are displaced within their own countries. They are the victims of persecution, human rights abuses, conflicts, and civil strife.

The term *refugee* has been defined by the UN Convention Relating to the Status of Refugees as a person who:

owing to well-founded fear of being persecuted for reasons of race, religion, nationality, membership of a particular social group or political opinion, is

1

Table 1.1.   Refugees and Asylum Seekers Worldwide (as of December 31, 2002)

Asylum Country	Total	Asylum Country	Total
Africa		Austria	30,900
Algeria	85,000*	Azerbaijan	11,400
Angola	12,000	Belarus	3,600
Benin	6,000	Belgium	30,300
Botswana	4,000	Bosnia and Herzegovina	34,200
Burundi	41,000	Bulgaria	1,200
Cameroon	17,000	Croatia	8,100
Central African Republic	50,000	Cyprus	1,800
Chad	16,000	Czech Republic	6,300
Congo-Brazzaville	118,000	Denmark	5,200
Congo-Kinshasa	274,000*	Finland	1,200
Côte d'Ivoire	50,000*	France	27,600
Djibouti	23,000	Georgia	4,200
Egypt	78,000*	Germany	104,000
Eritrea	3,000	Greece	1,800
Ethiopia	115,000*	Hungary	1,200
Gabon	20,000	Ireland	6,500
Gambia	10,000	Italy	5,200
Ghana	41,000*	Lithuania	200
Guinea	182,000*	Macedonia	2,700
Guinea-Bissau	7,000	Moldova	300
Kenya	221,000*	Netherlands	17,200
Liberia	65,000*	Norway	5,900
Libya	12,000	Poland	300
Malawi	13,000	Romania	100
Mali	4,000	Russian Federation	17,400
Mauritania	25,000*	Slovak Republic	4,500
Morocco	2,000	Slovenia	400
Mozambique	7,000	Spain	200
Namibia	26,000	Sweden	24,900
Nigeria	7,000	Switzerland	44,200
Rwanda	32,000	Turkey	10,000
Senegal	45,000*	Ukraine	3,600
Sierra Leone	60,000*	United Kingdom	79,200
South Africa	65,000	Yugoslavia	353,000
Sudan	287,000*	**TOTAL**	**859,900**
Swaziland	1,000		
Tanzania	516,000*	**THE AMERICAS AND THE CARIBBEAN**	
Togo	11,000	Argentina	2,700
Uganda	221,000*	Belize	1,000
Zambia	247,000*	Bolivia	400
Zimbabwe	10,000	Brazil	3,700
TOTAL	**3,029,000**	Canada	78,400
		Chile	400
EUROPE		Columbia	200
Albania	100	Costa Rica	12,800
Armenia	11,000	Cuba	1,000

(continued)

Table 1.1. *(continued)*

Asylum Country	Total	Asylum Country	Total
Dominican Republic	300	**MIDDLE EAST**	
Ecuador	9,100	Gaza Strip	879,000
Guatemala	700	Iran	2,208,500*
Mexico	4,000	Iraq	134,700
Panama	1,700	Israel	2,100
Peru	900	Jordan	155,000
United States	638,000**	Kuwait	65,000
Uruguay	100	Lebanon	409,000
Venezuela	1,100	Saudi Arabia	245,400
TOTAL	**756,500**	Syria	482,000
		West Bank	627,000
EAST ASIA AND THE PACIFIC		Yemen	81,700
Australia	25,000	**TOTAL**	**5,289,400**
Cambodia	300		
China	396,000	**SOUTH AND CENTRAL ASIA**	
Indonesia	28,700	Bangladesh	122,200*
Japan	6,500	India	332,300
Malaysia	59,000	Kazakhstan	20,600
Nauru	100	Kyrgyzstan	8,300
New Zealand	1,700	Nepal	132,000
Papua New Guinea	5,200	Pakistan	1,518,000*
Philippines	200	Tajikistan	3,500
South Korea	1,200	Turkmenistan	13,700
Thailand	336,000	Uzbekistan	38,000
Vietnam	16,000	**TOTAL**	**2,188,600**
TOTAL	**875,900**		

WORLD TOTAL			**13,000,000**

* Sources vary significantly.
** Where cases only were reported, the U.S. Committee for Refugees (USCR) approximates the number of individuals represented per case.
Source: World Refugee Survey 2003, USCR.

outside the country of his nationality and is unable or, owing to such fear, is unwilling to avail himself of the protection of that country; or who, not having a nationality and being outside the country of his former habitual residence as a result of such events, is unable or, owing to such fear, is unwilling to return to it.

The definition has been extended in Africa, through a convention approved by the Organization of African Unity, to cover any person who "owing to external aggression, occupation, foreign domination or events seriously disturbing public order in either part of or the whole country, is compelled to seek refuge outside his country of origin."

Table 1.2.   Principal Sources of Internally Displaced Persons (IDPs) (as of December 31, 2002)

This table identifies countries in which large numbers of civilians have been internally displaced by persecution, armed conflict, or widespread violence. Estimates of the number of internally displaced persons are often fragmentary and vary widely. This list includes more than 22 million people; the total number of IDPs may be much higher.

Sudan	4,000,000*	Kenya	230,000*
Columbia	2,500,000	Algeria	100,000–200,000*
Angola	2,000,000–3,500,000*	Zimbabwe	100,000–200,000*
Congo-Kinshasa	2,000,000*	Syria	170,000*
Iraq	1,100,000*	Liberia	100,000–150,000*
Burma	600,000–1,000,000*	Nepal	100,000–150,000*
Indonesia	600,000–1,000,000	Congo-Brazzaville	100,000*
Turkey	380,000–1,000,000*	North Korea	100,000*
Jordan	800,000	Ethiopia	90,000
Afghanistan	700,000*	Eritrea	75,000
Uganda	600,000–700,000*	Bangladesh	60,000*
Côte d'Ivoire	500,000–700,000*	Armenia	50,000
India	600,000	Nigeria	50,000*
Azerbaijan	576,000	Philippines	45,000
Sri Lanka	563,000	Gaza Strip and	
Burundi	400,000*	the West Bank	26,000
Russian Federation	371,000	Guinea	20,000*
Bosnia and		Croatia	17,000
Herzegovina	368,000	Mexico	12,000
Somalia	350,000*	Central African Republic	10,000
Lebanon	300,000	Macedonia	9,000
Cyprus	265,000	Haiti	6,000
Georgia	262,000	Senegal	5,000*
Yugoslavia	262,000*	Solomon Islands	4,000
Israel	250,000*		

*Sources vary significantly.
Source: World Refugee Survey 2003, U.S. Committee for Refugees.

Internally displaced persons (IDPs) are individuals who have left their homes because of persecution, civil war or strife, abuses of human rights, and similar causes but have not crossed an international border (see table 1.2). They also include people displaced by natural disasters and development programs. The *Guiding Principles on Internal Displacement* describe internally displaced persons as:

> persons or groups of persons who have been forced or obliged to flee or to leave their homes or places of habitual residence, in particular as a result of or in order to avoid the effects of armed conflict, situations of generalized violence, vi-

olations of human rights or natural or human-made disasters, and who have not crossed an internationally recognized State border.

Because refugee status inherently implies movements across international borders, a joint responsibility between international organizations and national governments has existed for some time and has been codified in international law. Primary responsibility for refugee protection and assistance rests with the UN High Commissioner for Refugees (UNHCR). In addition, the UN Relief and Works Agency for Palestine refugees in the Near East (UNRWA) provides education, health relief, and social services to Palestinian refugees in Lebanon, Syria, Jordan, the West Bank, and the Gaza Strip. Other UN agencies, such as the World Food Program (WFP), the UN Children's Fund (UNICEF), the UN Development Program (UNDP), the World Health Organization (WHO), and the International Labor Organization (ILO) are also called upon to provide expertise in matters related to their areas of interest. In addition, nongovernmental organizations (NGOs) have traditionally played an important role as a partner in the implementation of programs for refugees.

By contrast, the responsibilities of international organizations to internally displaced persons is less clearly defined, even if the displaced have fled for reasons that would have made them refugees had they crossed an international border. The mandate of the International Committee of the Red Cross (ICRC) extends to people internally displaced because of armed conflict. The UN Office for the Coordination of Humanitarian Affairs has established a small unit to "promote system wide improvements in the response to the needs of the internally displaced people (IDPs) as well as to provide targeted support to specific country situations." UNDP resident representatives have responsibility for coordinating assistance to the internally displaced in the field. However, no UN agency has a protection mandate for internally displaced that is comparable to UNHCR's mandate regarding refugees. UNHCR has extended its protection to IDPs in selected situations, particularly when refugee returnees mingle with IDPs during the repatriation process or when the secretary general specifically asks UNHCR to take on this role.

Refugees and displaced persons are not just of concern to international organizations. They are and should be of concern to all of us. Refugee situations, if left unresolved, can have serious consequences for:

- The Host Country. Most refugees have moved from one developing country to another, with a large portion coming from and going to countries that are among the least developed in terms of per capita income. Similarly, most IDPs are in developing countries as well. Often settling in the poorest areas of their host countries, the refugees can adversely affect local services, job markets, food costs, water supplies, and the environment.

- Regions in Conflict. Situations of forced migration can become explosive. The situation of Palestinian refugees, unresolved for more than forty years is a source of continuing disruption in the Middle East. Conflict has spread across borders in West Africa and the Great Lakes region along with the movement of refugees. The amelioration of most regional and internal conflicts in the world depends in part on a dignified and humane solution for refugees and displaced persons.
- The World Community. Refugees and displaced persons are people with skills to offer and contributions to make. They contribute in countless ways to the communities in which they settle and are a resource for the reconstruction of their home countries. Yet, too often, refugees and displaced persons remain in temporary arrangements, dependent on international assistance, and their potential remains unrealized.

Assistance to refugees and others of concern to the UNHCR costs more than the $1 billion spent per year by UNHCR itself (see table 1.3). Bilateral agencies, NGOs, and host governments spend untold millions more in the same effort. Of course, the greatest toll of unresolved refugee situations falls upon the refugees themselves, with women and children bearing the greatest costs—in deprivation and unproductive lives.

How many women and children are displaced today? Unfortunately, this question cannot be answered with adequate statistics. UNHCR has made valiant

Table 1.3.   Top 20 Donors to International Refugee Aid Agencies 2002*

Contribution in Millions of U.S. Dollars

United States	422.5	Canada	32.9
European Commission	138.7	Italy	26.1
Japan	124.1	Switzerland	23.6
Netherlands	78.5	France	13.9
Australia	70.9	Finland	13.6
United Kingdom	64.1	Belgium	10.7
Sweden	63.5	Ireland	8.5
Norway	58.0	Spain	6.1
Germany	43.5	Luxembourg	5.4
Denmark	41.6	Saudi Arabia	2.5

*The world's developed countries contribute most of the funding for programs that assist refugees. This table shows the amount of financial assistance provided during 2002 to three international agencies: UNHCR, IOM, and UNRWA. Many European countries contribute both through the European Commission as well as individually. Bilateral aid and aid provided through agencies such as the World Bank and the World Food Program that may benefit refugees are not included.

Sources: World Refugee Survey 2003, U.S. Committee for Refugees; UNHCR, IOM, and UNRWA.

efforts to collect demographic data on the gender and age of persons under its mandate, but in 2001 disaggregated data could be provided on only 8 million persons, 45 percent of the total under UNHCR's mandate (see table 1.4).[2]

The data on gender and age composition were better for refugees (62 percent) but there was a demographic breakdown on only 18 percent of the IDPs, returnees, and other groups under its care. Even when information is available on gender, age breakdowns are not available for 15 percent of the people. Data availability also differed by region. Whereas the gender breakdown for almost 70 percent of the population in the Eastern, Horn, and Great Lakes regions of Africa is known, data are available on less than 15 percent of the South Asian population.

These admittedly weak statistics provide some sense of demographic profile, however. Including all age groups, females represent 48.1 percent of the population. An estimated 11.6 percent of the population is children under the age of five and an additional 32.9 percent are of school age. An estimated 6.9 percent are sixty years of age and older. Overall about 70 percent of the population whose demographic profile is known to UNHCR is composed of women and dependent children.

Several mechanisms are used to enumerate refugees and displaced persons. According to the UNHCR *Handbook for Emergencies*, the most practical time to register refugees is on arrival, in conjunction, for example, with health screening. Reception centers are common, which allow incoming refugees to be registered and then transferred to a more permanent site. Such a system provides the advantage of being able to not only count arrivals but to obtain specific information about their health status, demographics, nutritional status, and so forth. The registration can also be used to distribute ration cards to the newcomers. When refugees stay for a protracted period, it is necessary to update the registration figures to take into account subsequent arrivals, departures, and births and deaths, a process that can be time-consuming and costly. UNHCR has made great strides in improving registration procedures, particularly in developing countries where it is primarily responsible for keeping track of refugees. Yet, even in countries where UNHCR is responsible for registration and data collection, the age and gender is known for only 75 percent of the refugees.

Where registration has not been feasible, a census may be taken using a number of different techniques: for example, counting the number of dwellings, if necessary through the use of aerial photography, or enumerating heads of households. Random sampling of the camp population is sometimes done in order to establish the demographic breakdown of the inhabitants. Census counts in refugee situations have been notoriously poor. Both overly high and overly low estimates of population can have adverse effects. In Somalia,

Table 1.4. Population of Concern to UNHCR by Gender and Age, End of 2001 (Estimates)

Region of asylum or residence	Female (thousands)						Male (thousands)						% Covered*
	0–4	5–17	18–59	60+ >	Other	Total	0–4	5–17	18–59	60+ >	Other	Total	
East, Horn, and and Great Lakes Region of Africa	193.1	387.0	461.9	24.0	144.6	1,210.5	193.3	425.2	452.2	24.1	118.7	1,213.5	68.8
North Africa	17.7	39.7	46.2	0.6	—	104.2	17.5	43.0	47.3	1.6	—	109.4	74.9
Southern Africa	15.6	32.1	47.3	1.2	169.7	265.8	16.3	36.4	75.5	1.3	207.2	336.8	38.3
West and Central Africa	68.7	163.5	193.0	25.4	0.0	450.5	63.4	162.0	189.3	22.7	0.0	437.4	47.2
Central Asia	7.1	13.2	15.5	1.2	50.0	87.0	6.9	17.1	20.5	2.0	69.3	115.8	21.1
East Asia and the Pacific	19.1	55.2	103.9	21.1	116.5	315.7	22.6	58.1	110.0	19.0	129.8	339.5	78.1
South Asia	46.2	164.1	233.0	19.2	35.3	497.7	47.8	167.0	233.5	24.9	35.3	508.5	14.6
South-West Asia	302.8	929.5	1,090.8	80.5	—	2,403.6	307.6	986.7	1,489.7	105.4	—	2,889.4	63.8
The Middle East	21.9	92.8	163.9	11.7	11.7	302.1	23.4	93.5	179.5	10.7	24.3	331.5	43.5

Region													
Central Europe and the Baltic States	0.8	3.3	7.5	1.0	4.7	17.3	1.0	4.4	17.4	0.5	6.0	29.3	44.7
Eastern Europe	17.7	89.4	312.9	195.6	627.4	1,243.1	18.9	88.2	261.1	145.2	553.6	1066.9	48.5
South-Eastern Europe													
Europe	32.0	155.7	473.2	163.6	1.1	825.6	34.6	164.4	441.5	117.3	1.0	758.7	45.5
Western Europe	4.1	9.5	24.8	0.8	738.4	777.6	4.9	15.5	69.7	0.6	1,179.3	1,270.0	13.0
Central America	1.4	5.0	5.5	0.6	0.9	13.4	1.3	5.0	7.0	0.6	1.0	14.9	61.5
North America and the Caribbean**	2.2	5.1	13.2	0.4	392.4	413.2	2.6	8.2	37.0	0.3	626.6	674.9	0.1
South America***	35.2	130.0	143.9	16.6	23.2	349.0	34.9	128.5	181.0	16.8	25.4	386.5	1.0
TOTAL	**957.3**	**2,659.3**	**3,795.8**	**606.7**	**1,494.3**	**9,513.4**	**971.1**	**2,824.3**	**4,333.6**	**537.9**	**1,579.2**	**10,246.1**	**45.5**

The figures here were extrapolated on the basis of disaggregated data for almost half of the population of concern to UNHCR.

*The percentage of the total population of concern for which the disaggregation by age and sex was available.

**Due to the small and nonrepresentative sample, the population has been estimated using the sex and age distribution of Western Europe.

***Due to the small and nonrepresentative sample, the population has been estimated using the sex and age distribution of Central America.

Source: UNHCR Statistical Yearbook, 2001.

for example, census counts for years overestimated the population and food rations were geared to the inaccurate count. Donors, convinced that the estimates were too high, decreased their contributions, leading to a reduction in the number of calories given in each ration. The assumption was that all families had more ration cards than members. This was not in fact the case, however. Those families with an accurate number of ration cards tended to suffer the most from this attempt to deal with the problems in the statistics.[3]

Since the majority of the world's refugees are in the least developed countries, refugee women and children naturally experience the same problems as other women and children in developing countries—poverty, lack of adequate food and safe drinking water, large families, high rates of child mortality, and relatively poor health. But added to these problems are the special ones associated with the refugee situation—the aftereffects of violence, persecution, and other traumatic events. For all refugees and displaced persons, the experience of becoming uprooted causes major changes in their lives. The impact for women and children is particularly poignant and, in some cases, traumatic, particularly when rape and sexual abuse become commonplace.

Yet, refugee and displaced women are much more than problems to be addressed. They can make substantial contributions to the development of their communities if provided the opportunity. At present, however, they are all too often an ignored, if not forgotten, resource.

The very fact that this book must begin with an estimate of the number of refugee and displaced women and children is testimony to continuing difficulty in effectively meeting the needs of this large population. While the statistic—that refugee women and their children constitute the majority of the refugee population—is widely used, its implications for programming and policy development have not been fully integrated into decision making.

This is not to say that there has been no progress in improving responses. During the past decade, greater policy attention has been brought to the issues of refugee women both within the UN system and many nongovernmental organizations. Yet much remains to be done, particularly in implementing policies to improve protection of refugee and displaced women. Thorough assessments of the needs of refugee and displaced women in specific countries and camps have not been made. Programs that respond effectively to the needs of refugee and displaced women have not been designed and implemented in many locations. Relative to men, refugee and displaced women still experience difficulties in gaining access to important services, such as income-generating projects and educational programs.

Perhaps most important, the significant contributions that refugee and displaced women can bring to bear in refugee situations have not been fully utilized. Without greater attention to both the needs and the potential contributions of refugee and displaced women and children, finding durable solutions to what in many places have become seemingly intractable humanitarian crises will be still more difficult.

NOTES

Full citations can be found in the select bibliography.

1. Author's journal, Site II, Thailand, November 1986.

2. In the mid-1990s, UNHCR could report demographic data on only 4 million persons under its mandate. These statistics are taken from the UN High Commissioner for Refugees, *Statistical Yearbook* (Geneva: UNHCR, 2001).

3. Angela Berry, "Refugee Women Case Study—Somalia," in *Working with Refugee Women: A Practical Guide*, ed. Ninette Kelly (Geneva: International NGO Working Group on Refugee Women, 1989).

Three Generations of Afghan Refugee Women, Iran. (UNHCR/A. Hollmann)

2

Refugee Women: Changing Roles

I am behaving strangely, I don't recognize myself. I am lost, I am scared, I don't communicate. That is not me. That is the refugee, as they call me. Without a home, without work, without any conditions for a normal life.[1]

Things are no longer as they used to be! You have to face up to things and adjust to the situation. We are refugees.[2]

For most refugee and displaced women, the experience of forced migration requires continuing response to change, including the need to cope with traumatic new circumstances. Forced to leave their homes because of persecution and violence, the refugee and displaced women must often cope with new environments, new languages, new social and economic roles, new community structures, new familial relationships, and new problems. At the same time, refugee and displaced women generally seek to reconstruct familiar lifestyles as much as is physically and socially possible. In a sense, then, refugee and displaced women are both agents of change and sources of continuity and tradition.

THE ROLE OF REFUGEE WOMEN IN FAMILY AND COMMUNITY

Displacement profoundly affects family and community structures, particularly when movements are involuntary responses to violence and abuses. Refugees and displaced persons move not because they wish to make better lives for themselves in other places but because they are forced to leave in order to seek safety elsewhere. The decision to move is often sudden, occurring

13

when families have exhausted all other remedies. Often, it is the disintegration of long-standing family and community resources that triggers the actual decision to flee. The uprooted realize that there is little to keep them in their home villages or towns because everything of importance has already been destroyed.

Upon becoming forced migrants, families must deal with many new living arrangements. Families lose one or more members. Fathers have died in fighting or have joined government or rebel military forces, leaving women as heads of households. Younger children and older relatives have died of hunger or disease upon the route to refuge. Others die soon after entering a refugee camp, too malnourished to survive even after help is offered. Still more family members succumb to epidemics that overcome crowded encampments in the first weeks and months of the crisis. Families are separated during flight, ending up in different camps or even countries of asylum. Traditional family patterns are thus disrupted, leaving refugees with neither intact nuclear families nor extended ones.

Once in camp, refugees and displaced persons often find themselves living with strangers. Used to small, stable villages, they must now cope with large encampments, sometimes with residents numbering in the tens or even hundreds of thousands. Members of different tribes and clans are expected to live side by side, even if they were traditional enemies. The layout of the encampments will often differ dramatically from the traditional village pattern. People are assigned to specific sites on a first-come, first-served basis. In other situations, refugees and displaced persons from rural areas move to urban centers either in a host country or in their own nation. They often do not know if their stay will be a short one, with return to their homes possible, or an extended one stretching into decades or even longer.

Some are transported thousands of miles away to resettlement countries with completely new cultures and languages. Others choose themselves to seek asylum in Europe or North America. They may pay criminal smuggling operations to get them there, or they may be trafficked by unscrupulous rings that promise them safety only to exploit their labor in brothels, sweatshops, or domestic labor. For those who come from developing countries, uprootedness means adapting to industrialized societies and the changes in economic and social systems that development brings.

For refugee women, these changes in family and community structures hold many ramifications. Uprootedness does not mean the same to all refugees:

> According to the depth of the gap differentiating the roles of women in the refugees' society of origin and in their country of resettlement, refugee women

may see a fundamental continuity between their experiences as women at home and those of the women native to their new communities, may come to question their own accustomed position in society as a result of having confronted alternative social patterns, or may experience a sense of loss as a result of the greatly different reality they now face.[3]

Yet, some issues appear to be common to most displaced women regardless of their location, even if they play out differently in different geographic contexts. First, the women remain responsible for most domestic activities whether in Third World camps or industrialized countries. It has been pointed out in studies in several camps that the day-to-day role of women often changes little while the same cannot be said for their husbands who no longer are able to cultivate fields or engage in outside employment. The frustrations experienced by the men can result in increased family tension and potential for violence. The domestic activities of women are time-consuming and, in the refugee context, potentially dangerous. For example, women usually collect water and firewood, both of which may sometimes be found in mine-infested areas.

Second, refugee women worldwide must cope with changes in family structures and roles. As noted above, refugee women often find themselves heads of households, with no husbands or older children to help in the support of the families. In such cases, women must either accept external help, generally through formal international or national assistance systems, or take on new economic roles to support their families by themselves. Too often, the very personnel responsible for assisting and protecting women and children instead exploit them, often requiring sex in exchange for aid.

In intact families, women must deal with the changes in male/female roles. Women in camps, as stated above, continue to be productive members of the family, but men often find themselves unable to fulfill their traditional productive roles. In industrialized societies, refugee families soon discover that families are unable to become self-supporting with only one person's wages. Women may enter the outside labor market in order to help the family gain financial independence. Refugee men may have a difficult time in accepting either the new role of women or their own inability to support fully their families. This loss of control may result in domestic violence, depression, and alcoholism.

Parent/child relationships also change as a result of uprooting. Younger members of the family are often able to adjust more quickly to the demands of the new situation. In both camps and industrialized societies, the younger people more easily pick up new languages—either the languages spoken by expatriates in the camps or the language of the new resettlement country. As a result, children including older girls are often able to assume economic roles that are unavailable to their parents. They also become the conduit for information and translators for their parents. In a sense, then, in the refugee situation the children may take on the typical role of the parent, being the force for socializing their elders to a new culture.

Intergenerational tensions often result from these changes in role. A Vietnamese refugee mother in France who spoke little French stated of her children: "They are ashamed of me, whereas at home nobody is ashamed of a member of the family, even one who is handicapped."[4]

Third, refugee women often experience a new role as principal maintainers of the traditional culture. The phenomenon of *purdah* is illustrative. It is perhaps the most striking attempt in a refugee situation to preserve what are seen as traditional values through the imposition of a specific role on women. *Purdah* is the Islamic practice that requires that women be secluded and kept separate from unrelated men. In Afghan refugee camps in Pakistan, the use of *purdah* was intensified and affected both rural and urban Afghan women who rarely had to practice it in their own homeland. In part, *purdah* is the result of the changed living situation in Pakistan. Women who lived among extended family members in rural Afghanistan were under fewer social restrictions than are women in the refugee villages because the latter are in closer proximity to large numbers of nonfamily members.

The intensification also reflected the fundamentalist strain of the Afghan resistance which opposed the liberalization of the role of women under the Soviet-dominated government in Afghanistan. Requiring strict observance of traditional practices among Afghan women became a symbol of the *jihad*, the holy war. As a graphic example of this situation, programs designed for refugee women were attacked in Pakistan, and staff working in these programs was threatened. Although the exact source of the attacks was unknown, it was widely believed that Afghan fundamentalists were responsible. The reverberations of this violence could be felt beyond the programs in Pakistan, of course, when the Taliban took over the Afghan state in the mid-1990s and imposed strict restrictions on all Afghan women.

Often, the role as "preservers of the culture" creates intergenerational conflicts for women. In many situations, older refugees are expected to be the preservers of the traditional culture while the younger generation copes with the new life. In some cases, this division of responsibility can lead to tensions between older and younger women, particularly when younger women are unwilling to assume the traditional roles.

Relations between older and younger generations of women may be especially affected by the refugee experience because of differences in the way each perceives the need to change or to maintain traditional ways of life. In a camp established for Afghan widows in Pakistan, new conflicts between groups arose. Many of the younger women, enjoying a first taste of freedom, wanted to go further in defying tradition. They spoke, for example, of the possibility of remaining single after having been widowed, rather than marrying the brothers of their late husbands as is customary. Older women, on the other hand, saw themselves—especially in the absence of men—as responsible for transmitting traditional practices to the younger generation, and viewed the younger women's rebellion against remarriage as a threat to the honorable fulfillment of their duty as Afghan, and Islamic, women.[5]

When given the opportunity, refugee women form effective new social systems that provide support for their members and the potential for helping others. Perhaps the most significant thing that one can say about refugee women is that they are resilient and inventive. In the face of these various demanding changes and often limitations in their roles, examples abound of women forming new communities and support systems: an Afghan women's center in Peshawar, women's farming cooperatives in Somalia, women's self-help groups in France, mutual assistance associations composed of women in the United States. These women-initiated ventures bode well for the fuller participation of women in the lives of their new communities if the resources they have to offer are more effectively tapped.

PARTICIPATION OF REFUGEE WOMEN

Popular participation has been defined in the development field as "active and meaningful involvement of the masses of people at different levels (a) in the decision-making process for the determination of societal goals and the allocation of resources to achieve them, and (b) in the voluntary execution of resulting programs and projects."[6]

While recognized as an important part of the development process, popular participation has lagged behind as an accepted part of refugee programming. As one commentator has noted, "refugee participation probably has the worst ratio of rhetoric to reality of any concept in the refugee field."[7]

Constraints on refugee participation include:[8]

- Reluctance of host country governments to permit refugees a role in decision making for fear of losing control and/or encouraging a sense of permanence among refugees involved in self-sufficiency efforts.
- Reluctance of nongovernmental organizations (NGOs), particularly those involved in emergency operations, to establish refugee participation as a

priority. NGOs often see community organization as an obstacle rather than support to their work.

- Barriers deriving from the differences in culture and values among host country nationals, expatriate staff, and the refugees themselves. These barriers include the more obvious language and cultural barriers that lead to misunderstandings and lack of communication, but also problems of racism, ethnocentrism, and discrimination.

- Conflicts within the refugee population. For example, conflicts between major ethnic groups or political factions can make refugee participation in decision making very difficult when the refugees are unable to agree upon their representatives. Moreover, traditional leaders may be absent or find that their roles and capabilities are limited by the changed circumstances in a refugee camp or settlement.

- Absence of qualified community organizers who can develop participatory programs that are effective in a refugee setting.

Despite these barriers, the benefits of refugee participation are clear. Participation enhances normal coping processes. Psychologists have pointed out that participation builds self-esteem, rebuilds self-confidence, reduces feelings of isolation, and reduces lethargy, depression, and despondency. Enhancing the capacity of refugees to cope with the aftereffects of the refugee-producing experience is an important part of the search for permanent solutions.

Participation is also cost-effective. Refugee participation can avoid many expensive mistakes. If refugees help with program design, the programs will usually be more effective than if they are designed by persons who are unfamiliar with the society and customs.

Participation leads to self-sufficiency. Maximizing refugee self-sufficiency is a key goal in most refugee assistance settings. To hasten self-sufficiency, refugees need to be involved in planning and decision making as soon as possible so as to avoid creation of dependency.

Finally, participation promotes protection. Internal protection problems are usually due as much to people's feelings of isolation, frustration, and lack of belonging to a structured society as they are to any other form of social problem. Refugee participation helps build the values and sense of community that reduce protection problems.

Even within a weak system, the absence of effective participation by refugee women stands out. The situation described in Mexico in 1987 is still not atypical:

> Women's participation is limited in all the groups [the major organizational structure in the camps], and especially so in those groups comprised predomi-

nantly of Indians. In a number of group meetings that we observed, we noted that women were present but were unable to speak Spanish (the common language in which meetings are conducted), and participated little. For their understanding of the subjects being debated, these women were dependent on the occasional and partial translations given to them.

In interviews, both men and women noted that language ability constituted the major impediment to women's participation. Nevertheless, upon closer observation, we concluded that language is not the principal obstacle. It is rather the shared view of men and women that women belong in the private sphere. The tradition in most Guatemalan families, and particularly in Indian families, is that women's views are aired in family circles, and within this context, have considerable weight.[9]

That this situation has not changed fundamentally could be seen in a 2002 assessment of implementation of the UNHCR *Guidelines on the Protection of Refugee Women*:

> Insufficient participation of refugee women in decision-making is a barrier to the full implementation of the *Guidelines*. In all the mission sites officials agreed that refugee consultations with both men and women were essential to effective camp governance and reported positive results from involving women in decision-making. But refugee women expressed frustration at their inability to act collectively to improve their living conditions. A narrow cadre of male political leaders or tribal elders dominated refugee leadership.[10]

Relief officials often point to cultural constraints in involving women in decision making, particularly where women had a limited role in the country of origin. Looking to women as decision makers under this circumstance, they argue, amounts to tampering with the culture of the group.

Yet women refugees prior to flight typically had opportunities to express their concerns and desires through their husbands and traditional support networks, as noted in the Guatemalan case study quoted above. Refugee women cite their role in familial decision making. A Vietnamese poem expressed the women's voices:

> We are the noi-tuong [home ministers]
> of our families.
> For centuries our women have participated in the decisions
> that influence all that is important
> to us as families
> and as a society.[11]

In refugee and displaced persons camps, however, many women are unable to participate through such mechanisms. Not only are their voices unheard if

alternative arrangements are not made, but perspectives that they have to offer cannot otherwise be factored into decision making. As will be discussed
in subsequent chapters, in the absence of adequate female representation in
decisions about such issues as food allocation, there will continue to be in-
equity in distribution systems as well as inefficiencies that could have been
overcome.

While there is much to be said for maintaining cultural values, replicating
traditional decision-making structures in a refugee or displaced persons situation may also be fraught with problems. In effect, the culture of the refugees
and displaced persons has already been tampered with. Social structures that
existed prior to flight often become fragmented or destroyed when people are
displaced. Deaths of natural leaders and family separations contribute to
strains on the social order. In these situations, it may be impossible to select
leaders on the basis of previous decision-making models.

Moreover, refugees sometimes live in a virtual time warp. The role of
women in their own countries may be changing dramatically (or might have
had the events leading to the population uprooting not occurred), but the
refugees remain isolated from these developments. Within Afghanistan, for
example, women had greater opportunity for education, employment, and political participation in the 1980s while many of the refugee leaders tried to
impose significant constraints on the role of women in villages in Pakistan.
To further complicate matters, Western agencies sometimes impose their concept of what traditional women's roles were or should be, even romanticizing
the dependency of women.

Information about such characteristics of refugee and displaced women as
their education, skills, family size, and composition is generally unavailable.
Yet, all of these factors contribute to the capacity of refugee women to be resources for their own families and their communities.

Participation of refugee women in program management has occurred in
a number of locations. For example, in Mexico some of the constraints on
the participation of Guatemalan women, referenced above, were overcome
through emergence of a refugee women's organization, Mama Maquin. One
of the aims of the organization was to select local representatives in different camps who would consult on assistance needs and participation of
women in projects. Mama Maquin worked with an Inter-Institutional Technical Committee for the Integral Development of Refugee Women composed of representatives of UNHCR, the Mexican government, and NGOs.
The first test of this working relationship was a survey of refugee women's
conditions in Chiapas. Mama Maquin was responsible for carrying out the
survey at the field level while the technical committee was to analyze the
findings and make recommendations about projects to be implemented by

NGOs and Mama Maquin. Preliminary findings showed the need for literacy training.[12]

Mama Maquin evolved over time to address new realities facing the Guatemalan refugees in Mexico:

> In the camps in Mexico, they promoted social change for women both in their families and societies by training refugee women in their rights and addressing gender discrimination in women's everyday lives. Mama Maquin, together with two other women's NGOs, Madre Tierra and Ixmuncane, gradually shifted their work from gender awareness to mobilizing women on behalf of the return movement. These NGOs continued to work with refugee women after they repatriated to Guatemala.
>
> This work began to transform gender relations for women who had previously been confined to the home. They learned to read and write, mastered Spanish, and were able to bond with one another. They organized to assert their rights, question gender roles, and challenge contentious issues such as women's right to land. Many found paid employment outside the home for the first time, and learned that they had options apart from being wives and mothers. They also played key roles in negotiating the terms of their repatriations.[13]

Unfortunately, the progress made in enhancing women's participation did not survive intact upon actual return to Guatemala. The refugee women were dispersed within the country, and they found it difficult to maintain the cohesion of the refugee camp. Further, much of their energies turned of necessity to coping with economic survival. Husbands also demanded a return to traditional social roles. Without the financial support of UNHCR, maintaining the organizational structure for promoting participation of women proved too difficult to accomplish.[14]

In a settlement in Zaire, female coordinators were elected by the camp population (all members, not just women). The role of the female coordinators was twofold. First, they participated in the distribution process within their residential areas. Second, they were responsible for what are termed "women's affairs"—ensuring that pregnant women receive prenatal care; encouraging vaccination of children; and providing basic health education. The female coordinator also attended meetings of the otherwise totally male leadership.[15]

The Khmer Women's Associations (KWA) in the camps along the Thai-Cambodian borders provided similar avenues for the input of women into decision making and implementation. The leadership of the KWA (which was generally chosen from the political parties that administered the camps) participated in discussions about issues that pertained to the camps' women and children. The KWA employed social workers who identified problems and needs within the camps, trainers who taught literacy classes and sewing/weaving classes, and teachers who ran day care centers for the children of women in training classes.

In a settlement in Zambia, a development planning management committee was established as the mechanism for refugee representation in decision making. At the time of an assessment by an international team, the committee contained seventeen members. Fifteen were refugees, representing the three nationalities found in the settlement (Angolans, Zairians, and Namibians). The group included two village chiefs who had the responsibility of informing the refugees of decisions but who had not formerly been involved in the decision-making process itself. The remaining two seats were occupied by Zambian community development workers who were employed by the government. Representatives of the voluntary agency responsible for increasing community development in the settlement, a partnership between Oxfam (U.K.) and the British Volunteer Service Organization, served ex officio in the meetings of the committee but had no vote. The committee included a number of women representatives who served at all levels in the structure. Women served as the cotreasurer of the committee and as heads of the education, health, and social and home economics committees.

CONCLUSION

The participation of refugee women in decision making and program implementation is a necessary step to ensuring that they are effectively protected, obtain assistance on an equal footing with men, have the opportunity to lead productive, secure, and dignified lives, and are enabled to provide assistance when needed to vulnerable groups. It is a theme that must run throughout all programming for refugee and displaced persons if the needs of the forced migrants are to be met and solutions found for these uprooted people.

NOTES

Full citations can be found in the select bibliography.

1. Julie A. Mertus, Jasmina Tesanovic, Habiba Metikos, and Rada Boric, eds. *The Suitcase: Refugee Voices from Bosnia and Croatia* (Berkeley: University of California Press, 1997), 170.
2. Annick Roulet-Billard, "First Person Feminine," *Refugees* 70 (1989): 26.

3. Sharon Krummel, *Refugee Women and the Experience of Cultural Uprooting* (Geneva: Refugee Service, World Council of Churches, n.d.).

4. Krummel, *Refugee Women*, 13.

5. Krummel, *Refugee Women*, 8.

6. UN Department of Economic and Social Affairs, *Popular Participation in Decision Making for Development* (New York: United Nations, 1975), 4.

7. Lance Clark, *Refugee Participation: Changing Talk into Action* (Washington, D.C.: Refugee Policy Group, 1987), 1.

8. Fred C. Cuny, *Refugee Participation in Emergency Relief Operations* (Washington, D.C.: Refugee Policy Group, 1987).

9. Patricia Weiss-Fagen and Arturo Caballero-Barron, *Refugee Participation Case Study: Guatemalans in Campeche and Quintana Roo, Mexico* (Washington, D.C.: Refugee Policy Group, 1987).

10. Women's Commission for Refugee Women and Children, *UNHCR Policy on Refugee Women and Guidelines on Their Protection: An Assessment of Ten Years of Implementation* (New York: Women's Commission for Refugee Women and Children, 2002).

11. John Tenhula, *Voices from Southeast Asia: The Refugee Experience in the United States* (New York: Holmes and Meier, 1991), 93.

12. Reported by the UNHCR Field Office in Mexico (1991).

13. "UNHCR's Approach to Gender Programming in Central America: A Case Study," in Women's Commission, *UNHCR Policy*, Annex IV.

14. Patricia Weiss-Fagen and Sally Yudelman, "Empowerment in the Shadow of War: Refugee Camp Experiences and Reintegration of Salvadoran and Guatemalan Women," in *Women and Women's Organizations in Post-Conflict Societies: The Role of International Assistance*, ed. Krishna Kumar (Washington, D.C. and Boulder, Colo.: Lynne Reinner, 2000).

15. Lance Clark, *Refugee Participation Case Study: The Shaba Settlements in Zaire* (Washington, D.C.: Refugee Policy Group, 1987), 13.

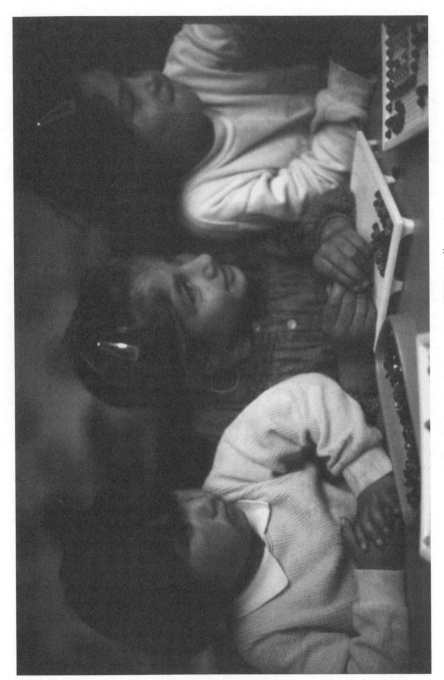

Asylum Seekers in Germany. (UNHCR/A. Hollmann)

3

A Safe Refuge? Protection of Refugee and Displaced Women

Pich Kola is 13 and from Indochina. She has been living in a refugee settlement for some three years. The camp is guarded but recently armed gangs from her country of origin have broken in to rob and terrorize the refugee population. Pich Kola's family hut is on the edge of the settlement so each night they move into the centre of the compound and sleep huddled together in the open. One night a gang entered the camp and went on a rampage which lasted for over five hours. Those refugees who could not pay the money demanded of them were simply killed by the attackers. Pich Kola hid in a fox hole. Her mother and sister were however not so fortunate: they were shot as they tried to flee.[1]

Protection is at the heart of the responsibility that the international community bears toward refugees and displaced persons. Forced migrants as a group are doubly disadvantaged and thus vulnerable to actions that threaten their protection. First, they are victims or potential victims of human rights abuses, conflicts, and other acts of aggression. Second, they are outside of their home communities and unable or unwilling to afford themselves of the protection that their own governments should provide.

There are two principal types of protection that forced migrants require. First, they need legal protection of their rights, particularly from return to situations in which they may be endangered. Second, they need physical protection to ensure their safety and security. Women share the protection problems experienced by all refugees and displaced persons. Along with all other refugees and displaced persons, women need protection against forced return to their countries or communities of origin; security against armed attacks and other forms of violence; protection from unjustified and unduly prolonged detention; the ability to enjoy their social and economic rights; and access to such basic items as food, shelter, and clothing.

In addition to these basic needs shared with all other refugees, refugee and displaced women and girls have special protection needs that reflect their gender and age: they need protection against sexual and physical abuse and exploitation and protection against sexual discrimination.

LEGAL PROTECTION

The instruments and organizations responsible for protection of refugees and internally displaced persons (IDPs) differ. Since the differences affect the extent of protection available to women in each category, they are addressed separately.

Refugees

The basic structures and legal instruments to ensure the protection of refugees were established fifty years ago. The Office of the UN High Commissioner for Refugees (UNHCR) was set up as of January 1, 1951, and the UN Convention Relating to the Status of Refugees was adopted in July 1951. The essential purpose of the convention was to provide a general definition of who was to be considered a refugee and to define his or her legal status. Paragraph 1 of the UNHCR's statute formally mandates the High Commissioner to provide international protection to refugees falling within his or her mandate, and to seek durable solutions to their problems.

The 1951 Convention was produced in the early days of the Cold War, largely to resolve the situation of the millions of refugees who remained displaced by World War II and fascist/Nazi persecution. At its core, this treaty substitutes the protection of the international community (in the form of a host government) for that of an unable or unwilling sovereign. Defining refugees as persons who were unable or unwilling to avail themselves of the protection of their home countries because of a "well-founded fear of persecution based on their race, religion, nationality, political opinion, or membership in a particular social group," the 1951 Convention included geographic (Europe) and time limitations (persons displaced before 1951) that were lifted in the 1967 Protocol. Since 1967, the refugee convention has been a universal instrument, applying to refugees worldwide.

According to the convention, states must refrain from forcibly returning (*refouling*) refugees to countries in which they would face persecution. States do not have the obligation to provide asylum or admit refugees for permanent settlement, and they may relocate refugees in safe third countries that are willing to accept them. The convention has been interpreted to require states to undertake status determinations, however, for asylum applicants at their frontiers or inside their territories in order to determine if they have valid claims to refugee protection. While the only obligation to a refugee is non-*refoulement*, in practice this has often meant admission and asylum in the host country.

The convention drafters recognized that among refugee populations would be found individuals whose actions made them undeserving of international protection. The so-called exclusion clauses of the convention set forth two major kinds of such individuals—human rights violators and serious criminals. Thus those who have committed a crime against peace, a war crime, a crime against humanity, or a serious nonpolitical crime are excluded from international protection.

The convention also sets out the rights of refugees who have been admitted unto the territory of another country. Fundamental human rights such as freedom of religion and access to courts are guaranteed to be at least those accorded to the citizens of the state hosting the refugee. Refugees lawfully residing in a host country are guaranteed public relief in this way as well. Rights regarding employment, property, elementary public education, and housing are accorded to refugees in a manner no less favorable than those accorded to citizens of other countries. In addition, the convention cannot be applied in a discriminatory way regarding race, religion, and country of origin.

The limits of a treaty focused on persecution as the cause of forced migration reverberated particularly in the developing world. In recognition of the actual forced movements occurring regularly in Africa, the Organization of African Unity (OAU) adopted the Convention Governing the Specific Aspects of Refugee Problems in Africa in 1969. While acknowledging the UN Refugee Convention as the basic and universal instrument regarding the protection of refugees, the OAU Convention broadened the definition and set out other important protection provisions. The expanded definition includes those who, "owing to external aggression, occupation, foreign domination or events seriously disturbing public order in either part or the whole of his country of origin or nationality, is compelled to leave his place of habitual residence in order to seek refuge in another place outside his country of origin or nationality."

The OAU explicitly forbids states from rejecting asylum seekers at the frontier. The grant of asylum is declared to be a peaceful and humanitarian act, not to be regarded as unfriendly by other states. The convention also establishes the importance of settling refugees at a reasonable distance from the frontier of their country of origin for security reasons. This regional treaty also states that no refugee shall be repatriated against his will. Most African states are parties to the OAU Convention.

In a similar vein, the Cartagena Declaration on Refugees expands the definition of protected refugees in the Latin American region. Like the OAU definition, it supports the 1951 Convention and adds protection to those who have fled their country "because their lives, safety, or freedom have been threatened by generalized violence, foreign aggression, internal conflicts, massive violation of human rights, or other circumstances which have seriously disturbed public order." It emphasizes that repatriation of refugees must be voluntary, and embodies principles for their protection, assistance, and reintegration. Although a nonbinding instrument, the declaration has been endorsed by the General Assembly of the Organization of American States, and most states in Central and Latin America apply the declaration's broader definition of a refugee as a matter of practice. Some have incorporated this definition into their own national legislation.

Legal Procedures and Criteria for the Determination of Refugee Status

Whereas in many developing countries assistance and protection is afforded on a presumptive basis to everyone from a given country who has crossed the border, in most industrialized countries and an increasing number of developing ones individuals must show that they meet the definition of a refugee. Women face special difficulties in obtaining refugee status. Two issues arise here: the grounds upon which someone is granted refugee status, and the process of establishing these grounds.

The UN Convention Regarding the Status of Refugees defines a refugee as a person who has a well-founded fear of being persecuted for reasons of race, religion, nationality, membership of a particular social group, or political opinion. Generally, to gain recognition as a refugee, asylum applicants (see table 3.1) must demonstrate that (1) the level of harm they have experienced rises to persecution, (2) their own government cannot or will not protect them from the harm, and (3) the persecution is based on one of the protected grounds included in the definition. These bases of persecution generally mirror the reasons that persons faced persecution during the Holocaust.

The claim to refugee status by women facing gender-based persecution presents special difficulties. Many cases involve women who are victims of domestic violence or who fear harsh or inhuman treatment because of having transgressed their society's laws or customs regarding the role of women.

Table 3.1. New Asylum Applications Submitted in Industrialized Countries, 1992–2001

Country of Asylum	1992	1993	1994	1995	1996	1997	1998	1999	2000	2001	Total
Australia	6,054	7,198	6,264	7,632	9,758	9,312	8,156	9,451	13,065	12,366	89,256
Austria	16,238	4,745	5,082	5,919	6,991	6,719	13,805	20,096	18,284	30,135	128,014
Belgium	17,647	26,882	14,353	11,420	12,433	11,788	21,965	35,780	42,691	24,549	219,508
Bulgaria	150	—	—	517	302	429	833	1,331	1,755	2,428	7,745
Canada	37,748	20,292	22,006	26,072	26,120	22,584	23,838	29,393	34,252	44,038	286,343
Cyprus	—	—	—	109	101	92	225	789	651	1,766	3,733
Czech Republic	817	2,193	1,188	1,413	2,156	2,098	4,082	7,285	8,787	18,087	48,106
Denmark	13,884	14,347	6,651	5,104	5,893	5,092	9,370	12,331	12,200	12,512	97,384
Estonia	—	—	—	—	—	—	23	21	3	12	59
Finland	3,634	2,023	839	854	711	973	1,272	3,106	3,170	1,651	18,233
France	28,872	27,564	25,964	20,415	17,405	21,416	22,375	30,907	38,747	47,291	280,956
Germany	438,191	322,599	127,210	127,937	116,367	104,353	98,644	95,113	78,564	88,287	1,597,265
Greece	1,850	813	1,303	1,312	1,643	4,376	2,953	1,528	3,083	5,499	24,360
Hungary	458	468	207	130	152	209	7,097	11,499	7,801	9,554	37,575
Iceland	13	3	—	5	4	6	19	17	24	52	143
Ireland	39	91	362	424	1,179	3,883	4,626	7,724	11,096	10,325	39,749
Italy	6,042	1,647	1,786	1,732	675	1,858	11,122	33,364	15,564	9,620	83,410
Japan	68	50	73	52	147	242	133	223	216	353	1,557
Latvia	—	—	—	—	—	—	58	19	4	14	95

(continued)

Table 3.1. New Asylum Applications Submitted in Industrialized Countries, 1992–2001 (continued)

Country of Asylum	1992	1993	1994	1995	1996	1997	1998	1999	2000	2001	Total
Liechtenstein	—	—	—	—	—	—	228	515	11	112	856
Lithuania	—	—	—	—	—	320	163	133	199	256	1,071
Luxembourg	—	—	—	394	240	427	1,709	2,912	628	686	6,996
Malta	403	—	—	148	75	65	165	85	71	116	1,128
Netherlands	20,346	35,399	52,573	29,258	22,170	34,443	45,217	42,733	43,895	32,579	358,613
New Zealand	771	347	426	675	1,317	1,495	1,972	1,528	1,551	1,601	11,683
Norway	5,238	12,876	3,379	1,460	1,778	2,271	8,373	10,160	10,842	14,782	71,159
Poland	592	819	598	843	3,211	3,533	3,373	2,955	4,589	4,506	25,019
Portugal	686	2,090	767	457	270	297	365	307	224	234	5,697
Republic of Korea	—	—	—	—	—	44	17	4	43	39	147
Romania	800	—	—	—	588	1,425	1,236	1,670	1,366	2,431	9,516
Slovakia	87	96	140	359	415	645	506	1,320	1,556	8,151	13,275
Slovenia	—	—	—	—	38	72	499	867	9,244	1,511	12,231
Spain	11,708	12,615	11,992	5,678	4,730	4,975	6,654	8,405	7,926	9,489	84,172
Sweden	84,018	37,583	18,640	9,047	5,753	9,662	12,844	11,231	16,303	23,515	228,396
Switzerland	17,960	24,739	16,134	17,021	18,001	23,982	41,302	46,068	17,611	20,633	243,451
Turkey	7,011	5,796	4,443	3,840	4,183	5,053	6,838	6,606	5,685	5,041	54,496
United Kingdom	32,300	28,000	42,200	55,000	37,000	41,500	58,487	91,200	98,900	92,000	576,587
United States	103,964	143,118	144,577	149,065	107,130	52,200	35,903	32,711	40,867	59,432	868,967
Total	**857,589**	**734,393**	**509,157**	**484,292**	**408,936**	**377,839**	**456,447**	**561,387**	**551,468**	**595,653**	**5,537,161**

Source: UNHCR Statistical Yearbook, 2001.

Even when they are able to demonstrate that the harm is so great it constitutes persecution and they have exhausted all efforts to receive protection from their governments, they are still faced with showing that the persecution is based on one of the protected grounds. As seen, gender is not one of the bases for persecution listed in the definition. And, as a UNHCR legal adviser has noted, "transgressing social mores is not reflected in the universal refugee definition."

Yet, examples abound of violence against women who are accused of breaking social mores or who are victimized because of their gender. The Taliban excesses against women are now well known. As recently as August 2002, Amnesty International reported its concern "at a decision . . . by a Sharia court of appeal in Nigeria, to uphold the sentence of death by stoning imposed on Amina Lawal, a young Nigerian woman who is alleged to have had a child out of wedlock."[2] The same year a Pakistani court also sentenced a woman to stoning death for adultery, although she claimed to have been raped, but in this case, the court of appeal overturned the conviction citing that the state should not punish people forced into adultery.[3]

Even more of a problem are situations in which women flee their country because of severe sexual discrimination either by official bodies or in local communities. Protection from sexual discrimination is a basic right of all women and is enshrined in a number of international declarations and conventions. While the universal right to freedom from discrimination on grounds of sex is recognized, and discrimination can constitute persecution under certain circumstances, the dividing line between discrimination and persecution is not a clean one. Discrimination can take on a number of forms. In some cases it is the fear of ostracism or retaliation not because of one's own actions but because of having been the victim of a crime carrying a social stigma, such as rape, that causes a woman to flee.

Women who are the targets of military attacks may also find difficulty in showing that they are victims of persecution rather than random violence. Similarly, women victimized because of the political activities of a male relative often have trouble demonstrating their claim to refugee status. Yet, in many conflicts, attacks on women are a planned part of a terror campaign. As one Somali woman described the war in her country:

> The war in Somalia is an anarchist war. It is a war on the women. Any woman between the ages of eighteen and forty is not safe from being forcibly removed to the army camps to be raped and violated. And that's only the beginning. If her husband finds out, he kills her for the shame of it all; if they know that he has found out, they kill him, too; if he goes into hiding instead, and she won't tell where he is, they kill her.

Similar stories have been told of the civil conflicts in Mozambique, Guatemala, and Eritrea.[4] The use of rape as a mechanism for ethnic cleansing came to international attention in Bosnia and Rwanda. As Human Rights Watch described:

> During the Rwandan genocide, thousands of women were targeted by Hutu militia and soldiers of the former government Armed Forces of Rwanda on their genocidal rampage. Tutsi women were individually raped, gang-raped, raped with objects such as sharp sticks or gun barrels, held in sexual slavery or sexually mutilated. These crimes were frequently part of a pattern in which Tutsi women were subjected to sexual violence after they had witnessed the torture and killings of their relatives and the looting and destruction of their homes.[5]

These acts prompted the tribunals created to address war crimes and crimes against humanity in these countries to include rape in its indictments. The Statute of the International Criminal Court expressly names rape and forced pregnancy as crimes against humanity when they are part of a widespread or systematic attack directed against a civilian population.[6]

Recognizing that gender is not part of the refugee definition, but unwilling to open up debate on the convention, the European Parliament urged in 1984 that women fearing cruel or inhumane treatment as a result of seeming to have transgressed social mores should be considered a "social group" for purposes of determining their status. In the Note on Refugee Women and International Protection submitted to the Forty-first Session of the Executive Committee in 1990, the High Commissioner also encouraged governments to take this step, noting:

> in light of the increasingly universal character of the United Nations Convention on the Elimination of All Forms of Discrimination Against Women, severe discrimination, in disregard of this Convention, may justify the granting of refugee status in line with the reasoning [of the European Parliament]. In order to facilitate the task of determining refugee claim of persons who are in such a situation, it is important that decision-makers involved in the refugee status determination procedures have at their disposal background material and documentation describing the situation of women in countries of origin, particularly regarding gender-based persecution and its consequences.[7]

In its 2002 *Guidelines on Gender-Related Persecution*, UNHCR reiterated: "Though gender is not specifically referenced in the refugee definition, it is widely accepted that it can influence, or dictate, the type of persecution or harm suffered and the reasons for this treatment. The refugee definition, properly interpreted, therefore covers gender-related claims. As such, there is no need to add an additional ground to the 1951 Convention definition."[8]

Several governments as well as UNHCR have issued guidelines or regulations to guide asylum determinations in this area.[9] They have touched on all three issues discussed above: the level of harm, the failure of state protection, and the nexus between the persecution and one of the grounds cited in the definition.

Persecution is generally defined to include a wide range of harms that may be detrimental to the safety and well-being of the woman. One court held: ". . . what conduct may amount to persecution is a question of degree. At one end of the scale there may be arbitrary deprivation of life, torture, and cruel, inhumane and degrading punishment or treatment. In such a case the conduct may be so extreme that one instance is sufficient. But less serious conduct may not amount to persecution unless it is persistent."[10] The harm need not be physical. A U.S. court case often cited in gender guidelines held that "the concept of persecution is broad enough to include governmental measures that compel an individual to engage in conduct that is not physically painful or harmful but is abhorrent to that individual's deepest beliefs."[11]

Some forms of persecution are in themselves gender-specific. The U.K. guidelines note that "gender-specific harm may include *but is not limited to* sexual violence and abuse, female genital mutilation, marriage-related harm, violence within the family, forced sterilisation, and forced abortion."[12] According to one report on sexual torture, the methods of torture can consist of:

Either hetero- or homosexual rape; the rape of women by the use of specially trained dogs; the use of electric currents upon the sexual organs; mechanical stimulation of the erogenous zones; manual stimulation of the erogenous zones; the insertion of penis-shaped objects into the body-openings (these can be made of metal or other materials to which an electrical current is later connected, are often grotesquely large and cause subsequent physical damage, and are used on both male and female victims); the forced witnessing of "unnatural" sexual relations; forced masturbation or to be masturbated by others; fellatio and oral coitus; and finally, the general atmosphere of sexual aggression which arises from being molested, from the nakedness, and from the lewd and lecherous remarks and threats of sexual aggression made to the prisoner and his or her family and threats of the loss of ability of reproduction and enjoyment in the future.[13]

The guidelines generally make a distinction as to the perpetrator of the persecution in determining whether the applicant is justified in being unable or unwilling to accept the protection of her home country. If the persecution is carried out by governmental authorities—state actors—"it follows that there is a failure of State protection." In many gender-persecution cases, however, the harm is carried out by nonstate actors—family members, armed elements who are not sanctioned by the government, even community members seeking to hold up social norms. Some countries do not recognize persecution by nonstate actors as coming within the refugee definition. Germany and France, for example, limit grants of asylum to those fearing persecution at the hands of state authorities. When nonstate actors are recognized, as they are in many other countries, the asylum applicant must demonstrate a failure of the state to provide protection from the nonstate actor.

The British guidelines note, "the State of origin is not expected to provide a guarantee against all risk of persecution, rather the level of protection to be expected is a practical standard in keeping with every state's primary duty to provide protection to those within its jurisdiction."[14] The guidelines emphasize, however, that state protection must be real. Just because there are laws on the book does not mean that protection is available to women. A landmark British case held that "it was useless for Mrs. Islam, as a woman, to complain to the police or the courts about her husband's conduct. On the contrary, the police were likely to accept her husband's allegations of infidelity and arrest her instead. The evidence of men was always deemed more credible than that of women. If she was convicted of infidelity, the penalties could be severe. Even if she was not prosecuted, as a women separated from her husband she would be socially ostracised and vulnerable to attack, even murder, at the instigation of her husband or his political associates."[15] In one particularly egregious case of domestic violence, the applicant tried to flee to another part of Guatemala to escape her husband, but he found her and increased the severity of the abuse. A Canadian case held: "An internal relocation alternative must offer reasonable longevity and be a substantive durable alternative to international protection through asylum. An asylum seeker must not be 'punished' for not choosing internal relocation in the past. There is no duty upon an asylum seeker to 'run and hide.'"[16]

The most difficult issue to overcome in gender-based cases is the nexus between the harm suffered and one of the protected grounds. As recommended by the European Parliament above, these cases often try to tie the persecution to the applicant's "membership in a particular social group." UNHCR guidelines issued in 2002 defined social group as: a particular social group is a group of persons who share a common characteristic other than their risk of being persecuted, or who are perceived as a group by society. The characteristic will often be one which is innate, unchangeable, or which is otherwise fundamental to identity, conscience or the exercise of one's human rights."[17]

The guidelines attempt to reconcile differing state practice. Social groups are usually defined as having certain immutable characteristics (such as gender) that the members cannot change. Alternately, the characteristics are so fundamental to their identity, their human dignity or conscience that they ought not to be required to change them. The social group cannot, however, be defined by the persecution suffered—that is, girls fearing female genital mutilation (FGM) are not a social group if the FGM is the persecution that is feared. But, as the Canadian guidelines emphasize, "the fact that the particular social group consists of large numbers of the female population in the country concerned is *irrelevant (sic)*—race, religion, nationality, and political opinion are also characteristics that are shared by large numbers of people."[18]

Different courts, even within the same countries, have taken different stances on the definition of a social group in gender-persecution cases. The U.K. House of Lords, for example, found that two Pakistani women who fled because of domestic violence in Pakistan (Islam v SSHD; R v IAT ex parte Shah) were members of a particular social group. At about the same time, the U.S. Board of Immigration Appeals (BIA) held in a similar case that a Guatemalan woman (Matter of R-A-) who, they said, suffered severe persecution at the hands of her husband, was not a member of a social group. The BIA held that the husband did not commit violence against other women, only his own wife. The U.S. case was subsequently vacated while the Justice Department issued new regulations on social group. The R-A- case seemed at odds with earlier gender-based decisions of the BIA, including a landmark case in which a woman fearing female genital mutilation was granted asylum. As of April 2003, the new regulations have not been issued.

Other common reasons that women suffer persecution relate to religion and political opinion. A woman may face serious harm because she is unwilling to practice religion as the authorities of her country require. These cases generally involve a refusal by the woman to follow the behaviors that religious leaders say are required of all adherents—for example, wearing the veil or other garments deemed proper for women. As the U.K. guidelines state: "Failure to abide by the behavioural codes set out for women may be perceived as evidence that a woman holds unacceptable religious opinions regardless of what she actually believes about religion."[19] In theocracies, opposition to these behaviors may also be, or be seen as, expressions of political opinion. As one expert on international refugee law argues: "In the 1951 Convention, 'political opinion' should be understood in the broad sense, to incorporate, within substantive limitations now developing generally in the field of human rights, any opinion on any matter in which the machinery of State, government, and policy may be engaged."[20] In addition to opposition to social norms upheld by the state, women may be persecuted for their opposition to laws and practices that discriminate against them or make it difficult for them to support themselves and their children.

Even where the basis for persecution would clearly fall into one of the defined areas, women face special problems in making their case to the authorities, particularly when they have had experiences that are difficult and painful to describe. The female victim of sexual torture may be reluctant to speak about it, particularly to a male interviewer. Rape, even in the context of torture, is seen in some cultures as a failure on the part of the woman to preserve her virginity or marital dignity. She may be shunned by her family and isolated from other members of the community. Discussing her experience becomes a further source of alienation.

The very delicate and personal issues arising from sexual abuse require the physical presence of officials who are trained and sensitive to the needs of refugee women. In most instances it requires female staff members who can communicate with victims about their personal experiences. Women are too often underrepresented in UN bodies working with refugees. They are also underrepresented in many government bureaucracies that conduct interviews for determining refugee status.

Sometimes, women who arrive as part of a family unit are not even interviewed or are cursorily interviewed about their experiences, even when it is they rather than their husbands who have been the targets of the persecution. A wife may be interviewed primarily to corroborate the stories told by her husband; if she is unaware of the details of her husband's experiences (for example, the number of her husband's military unit), the entire testimony may be discounted as lacking in credibility. Yet, in many cultures, husbands do not share many details about military or political activities with their wives.

These problems are noted in the various guidelines developed for asylum adjudicators. They generally recommend a nonconfrontational environment for hearing women's claims, with female adjudicators and interpreters. If it appears that the presence of family members will make it unlikely that the applicant will tell her story in full, she should be interviewed on her own. Interviewers should have gender-sensitive training and be familiar with the conditions for women in the country of origin, as well as the experiences that women may have undergone in leaving their countries and seeking asylum.

A further legal problem affecting refugee women is the actual status they are granted by a country of asylum. In most countries, family members who are accompanying or join a person who is granted refugee status are granted the same status. This provision is not seen in all places, however. Nor is conferral of refugee status automatic for spouses and children who follow a refugee to a country of asylum. Family reunification is not a right conferred on refugees by the UN Convention; it is a recommended practice that leaves much to the discretion of individual states. While many allow family members to immigrate, a number of countries grant family members a residency status that provides less protection against deportation than does refugee status. Should the family break up, the wife (who is more often the person to be joining the one granted refugee status) may find herself without any protection from forced return.

This section has highlighted a number of steps that can be taken to improve the legal protection of refugee women. To summarize, UNHCR, governments, and NGOs should:

- Reaffirm the political, economic, social, cultural, and civil rights of refugee and displaced women, with due regard for relevant international legal instruments, such as the Convention on the Elimination of all Forms of Discrimination against Women.
- Consider women fearing persecution or severe discrimination on the basis of their gender to be a social group for the purposes of determining refugee status.
- Inform refugee women of their rights and the benefits to which they are entitled.
- Ensure that immigration officials have access to comprehensive "country of origin information" that details the situation of women.
- Provide training to asylum officers doing status determinations regarding the interviewing and assessment of the claims of women.
- Employ women as interviewers and interpreters for purposes of determining status.

Internally Displaced Persons

The legal and institutional arrangements for protecting internally displaced persons are far more rudimentary than those for refugees. Until about a decade ago, there was little in the way of international protection for internally displaced persons, who were seen to be under the sovereign authority of their own governments. There has been growing recognition, however, that many internally displaced persons are in the same situation as refugees—unwilling or unable to obtain real protection from their own government. This has led to increased willingness to offer international assistance and protection, generally through peaceful means but on occasion through military force. The international community has intervened militarily in Northern Iraq, Somalia, Haiti, Kosovo, and East Timor, citing in part the concern that the severe plight of internally displaced persons threatened to become a refugee crisis that would threaten the security of neighboring countries.

International human rights and humanitarian law have growing salience in defining sovereignty to include responsibility for the welfare of the residents of one's territory. To quote Francis Deng, the representative of the UN Secretary General on Internally Displaced Persons, and his colleague Roberta Cohen, in arguing for greater international attention to internally displaced persons,

> Since there is no adequate replacement in sight for the system of state sovereignty, primary responsibility for promoting the security, welfare and liberty of populations must remain with the state. At the same time, no state claiming legitimacy can justifiably quarrel with the commitment to protect all its citizens against human rights abuse. . . . Sovereignty cannot be used as justification for the mistreatment of populations.[21]

Being internally displaced is *not* a legal status. Unlike refugees, the internally displaced have not left the country whose citizens they normally are. As such, they remain entitled to the same rights that all other persons in their country enjoy. These rights derive not only from national law but also from various international instruments: human rights conventions and, to the extent displacement is caused or affected by war, the Geneva Conventions. Applying these international laws to the situation of internally displaced persons, the *Guiding Principles on Internal Displacement*, developed in the late 1990s, sets forth the major rights of the internally displaced and the responsibilities of sovereign authorities to such individuals prior to and during displacement. The *Guiding Principles* also look to international refugee law by analogy for guidance in certain situations.

Although the principles do not have legal force themselves, they set standards that guide governments and insurgencies regarding their conduct toward civilians before, during, and following displacement. This consolidation and focusing of international law regarding the internally displaced has been adopted into domestic law by nations such as Colombia and Georgia. Important gaps in the protection framework for internally displaced persons continue to exist, however, as the human rights laws and the Geneva Conventions are laws of general applicability that were not specifically designed to address the full range of problems that the internally displaced face.

The *Guiding Principles* are organized around different phases of displacement, each raising somewhat different issues in terms of the rights of the IDPs and obligations of government and the international community. First is protection from displacement. The most effective way to address internal displacement is to avoid conditions that might compel people to leave their homes against their will. Displacement is prohibited, no matter what the circumstances, when it seeks to alter the ethnic, religious, or racial composition of particular areas. This absolute prohibition applies to ethnic cleansing, apartheid, and forcible displacement used as a collective punishment. Although protection against other forms of displacement is not absolute, states violate their obligations if they displace persons arbitrarily, that is, without compelling reasons strictly required to protect national security, public order, public health, or similar public interests.

Protection against arbitrary displacement exists in times of war as well as peace. As a general rule, warring parties are prohibited from forcing civilians to move unless they can demonstrate that the security of the affected population or imperative military reasons so demand. Since displacement should be the exception and not the rule in combat, the burden is on the warring party to make the case that population movements are justified. The Geneva Conventions specify, "the displacement of the civilian population shall not be ordered for reasons related to the conflict unless the security of the civilians involved or imperative military reasons so demand."[22]

In some situations—for example, during armed conflict—moving people from their homes may be the best and most humane way to safeguard their physical integrity. Wherever possible, however, alternatives to displacement should be explored to ensure that displacement occurs only as a last resort. The *Handbook on Implementing the Guiding Principles*, disseminated by the United Nations, emphasizes: "One of the best ways to protect people from arbitrary displacement is to involve them in the decisions about their future. Sometimes, consultations with the populations to be displaced will identify some possible alternatives to displacement. . . . Other times, consultations will make clear that there are no alternatives. Often, people will move voluntarily if they understand the reasons that the movements are necessary and feel that they have been part of the decision."[23] Providing opportunities for women to participate in the consultation process is essential. The *Handbook* explains: "Women's participation in planning efforts will help ensure not only their own safety and well-being but it increases the likelihood that issues pertaining to the broader family—for example, the safety and education of children or the availability of food and cooking supplies—will get needed attention."

The *Guiding Principles* further set out rights of IDPs during displacement. Internally displaced persons are particularly vulnerable during the period of displacement, making it essential to ensure their protection from military attacks and forced recruitment, inhumane or degrading treatment, detention, internment, forced separation from families, and other violations of human and civil rights. Addressing the most fundamental right that an internally displaced person shares with every human being, the *Guiding Principles* emphasize that no one should be arbitrarily deprived of his or her life.

Recognizing the often dire situation in which internally displaced persons find themselves, the *Guiding Principles* give special attention to the need to protect them from genocide, murder, summary or arbitrary executions, and enforced disappearances that result in death. There is also prohibition against torture, cruel, inhuman, and degrading treatment. Even in emergency situations, responsible authorities may not violate or permit the violation of this right. Nor may internally displaced persons be subject to rape, mutilation, gender-specific violence, forced prostitution, or other indecent assault. The *Guiding Principles* also call for protection from slavery, including sale into marriage, sexual exploitation, and forced labor of children.

Except under emergency circumstances, people have the right to seek safety wherever they are able to find it. They have the right to remain where they are if that is their choice. They have the right to move to another part of the country. They have the right to leave their country altogether and seek asylum elsewhere. Particularly important for the internally displaced, the *Guiding Principles* make clear there should be no internment or confinement to a camp unless exceptional circumstances make it absolutely necessary and only while the exceptional circumstances continue. Camps may be established as a mechanism for aiding and protecting internally displaced persons, but these facilities must be open.

Internally displaced persons also have the right to be protected against forcible return to or resettlement in any place where their life, safety, liberty, and/or health would be at risk. Just as the principle of non-*refoulement* (the prohibition against forced return to their home countries) is the most important right for refugees, protection from forced returns is also essential for protecting internally displaced persons. On the other hand, IDPs have the right to return voluntarily, in safety, and with dignity, to their homes or to resettle voluntarily in another part of the country. This right is a logical extension of the right to liberty of movement and freedom to choose one's residence. Respect for this right is particularly important when the conditions that caused the displacement cease and internally displaced persons may leave their place of refuge.

The *Guiding Principles* further spell out the economic, social, and cultural rights that apply particularly to the displaced. Drawing upon human rights and humanitarian law, the *Guiding Principles* make clear that competent authorities have the responsibility to provide internally displaced persons with or ensure safe access to basic assistance. Regardless of whether they live in camps or are dispersed in cities and rural areas, at a minimum, internally displaced persons must have access to essential food and potable water, basic shelter and housing, appropriate clothing, and essential medical services and sanitation. The *Guiding Principles* emphasize the importance of involving women in planning and distributing the basic supplies afforded internally displaced persons by right. Excluding women, the *Handbook* points out, is a violation of their human rights.

Although the *Guiding Principles* spell out a meaningful standard for the protection of IDPs, the capacity to ensure that their rights are protected is far more limited. Unlike refugees, there is no international organization specifically mandated to protect the rights of IDPs. National governments retain the principal responsibility for protecting their citizens. The problem comes when sovereign states are unwilling or unable to fulfill their responsibilities. The *Guiding Principles* spell out that: "International humanitarian organizations and other appropriate actors have the right to offer their services in support of the internally displaced. Such an offer shall not be regarded as an unfriendly act or an interference in a State's internal affairs and shall be considered in good faith. Consent thereto shall not be arbitrarily withheld, particularly when authorities concerned are unable or unwilling to provide the required humanitarian assistance." Too often, however, international humanitarian organizations do not offer their services, or because of risks to their safety and security, are unable to reach the IDPs in most need.

Nevertheless, steps can be taken to improve legal protection of internally displaced persons, including:

- bringing greater public attention to the plight of internally displaced persons, focusing on the situation of women and their dependents;
- engaging human rights institutions, including the UN human rights system and NGOs, along with relief and development agencies in exposing cases where governments refuse to provide safety, food, clothing, medicine, and other essentials to their displaced populations; and
- disseminating and providing training on the *Guiding Principles on Internal Displacement*.

REGISTRATION AND DOCUMENTATION

Registration is a further issue that undermines legal protection of refugee and internally displaced women alike. As early as 1986, the problems that can be encountered when refugee women do not have their own documentation were reported in a study prepared for the Economic Commission for Africa:

During the late 1950s and early 1960s, many Rwandese refugees fled to Uganda en masse. In time, they integrated into the local population and became self-reliant, so that UNHCR assistance was gradually phased out. The recent disturbances, however, have uprooted many resettled refugees. Many have been widowed, and others separated or deserted. Thus, UNHCR has found it necessary to reestablish relief assistance services. In order to qualify for these services, however, refugees were required to present their identification cards, but most of the displaced women never had such cards. A complicated and lengthy process resulted, whereby refugees had to prove their status which delayed access to urgently needed relief assistance. The problem of lack of documents is widespread and serious and requires an urgent solution.[24]

Failure to provide for registration creates many psychological and practical problems, particularly for refugee and displaced women who are the primary caregivers in their families. Registration is necessary not only to establish legal standing, age, and nationality but also to obtain assistance in many locations.

The *Guiding Principles* emphasize the responsibility of authorities to issue internally displaced persons all documents needed to exercise their legal rights, including passports, personal identification documents, birth certificates, and marriage certificates. If internally displaced persons need to replace lost or destroyed documents, governments must facilitate the issuance of new ones.

UNHCR has made progress during the past decade in designing and pilot-testing new registration systems for refugees who cross international borders. Referred to as Project Profile, the new system would strengthen UNHCR's field capacity to support more effective registration and documentation programs. UNHCR has described the benefits of a functioning registration system:

Adequate registration, including the issuance of documentation, is a prerequisite for the legal and physical protection of refugees. First, accessing assistance and services in implementing a range of civil rights, including those which are protection-related (tracing, family reunification, freedom of movement, right not to be returned or expelled) flow from acknowledged and recorded refugee identity. Registration also ensures that each family member is independently recognized, which has important implications particularly for women and for children. Second, early and proper identification reduces multiple registration and the use of fraudulent identity papers, particularly for the purpose of obtaining additional relief items. Third, registration is necessary to plan and implement refugee programmes, to manage camps and to target protection and assistance activities at the field level. Fourth, States, UNHCR and operational partners require reasonably accurate population data to allocate resources, to monitor delivery and to evaluate interventions. Fifth, reliable registration information is necessary for the identification, planning and expeditious implementation of durable solutions.[25]

Yet, inadequate processes for registering and providing documentation continue to be a problem. On the tenth anniversary of the issuance of UNHCR's *Guidelines on Protection of Refugee Women*, which emphasized the importance of registration, an evaluation found:

> In the majority of camps, refugee registration cards are still essentially ration cards. Thus, where there is no food assistance, refugees go unregistered, as in the case of Afghan refugees in Pakistan after food assistance was eliminated in 1995. Neither Afghans who came thereafter, nor those born in Pakistan after 1995, are likely to have any personal documentation at all, much less proof of refugee status.

Sometimes, countries of asylum register and provide documentation to the male head of a refugee household but offer no proof of residency to other family members. Should the men abandon their families or otherwise not be present, it is difficult if not impossible for their wives to prove that they are legally in the country.

Registration of marriages and births is a further problem for many refugee families. In some countries, no procedures exist for formally registering marriages and births that take place in refugee or displaced persons camps. In other countries, registration can take place in camps but there are no procedures for the spontaneously settled. Alternatively, urban refugees can register their children but there are no procedures for those in rural settings. In still other cases, the procedures are in place but refugees and displaced persons are afraid to make use of them for fear of coming to the attention of the authorities.

Some countries of asylum do not even recognize as legal a marriage that takes place in a refugee camp.

> After two years of camp life Pilar married a fellow refugee. Her marriage is however not recognized under the law of the country of asylum and there is no system of registration of marriages in the settlement where they live. The child born to Pilar last year is considered illegitimate.[26]

Statelessness is a problem facing many refugee children. In a number of situations, there are conflicting national laws concerning the attribution of nationality. A country of asylum may hold that a child born on its territory cannot have its nationality if the child's parents are of a different nationality. The country of the parent's origin may hold, however, that the children are ineligible for its nationality if born on another country's soil.

Even where documentation can be legally obtained, constraints in registering exist for refugee women, particularly women heads of households. These
constraints include physical and logistical difficulties in reaching the authorities responsible for registration, particularly in cultures that do not permit
women to interact with strangers, and lack of access by single women and
women heads of households to information about benefits to which they are
entitled.

PHYSICAL SECURITY

While conflict and uprooting can present problems of safety to all refugees
and displaced persons, women and their dependents are particularly vulnerable. Their physical security is at risk both during flight and after they have
found supposed safety in an asylum country or as an IDP. Protection problems
can also be found after refugee and displaced women find durable solutions,
such as repatriation or resettlement. (These latter issues are discussed in chapters 6 and 7.)

Trying to understand, anticipate, and prevent sexual violence in these situations is difficult at best. As one report notes of gender-based violence
(GBV):

> Sexual violence can be capricious or random—the "spoils of war"—resulting
> from the breakdown in social and moral systems. Indeed, it is likely that this
> kind of "collateral" GBV is an element of all wars. In addition, sexual violence
> may be systematic, for the purposes of destabilizing populations and destroying
> bonds within communities and families; advancing ethnic cleansing; expressing
> hatred for the enemy; or supplying combatants with sexual services.[27]

Flight

> We traveled for six days to get to Belgrade. The planes shelled the convoy. Peo-
> ple were killed, entire families. Sometimes we had to get off the road, hide in
> the forest, or go through the field to avoid the shellings.[28]

The decision to leave one's home country is a difficult one at best. Generally a combination of factors finally leads to a determination that flight is the
only possibility. Refugee women are not always part of that decision-making
process, however. As one Afghan woman described, "My husband came in
and said, 'we're leaving. Women prepare our things. We are taking as little as
possible. All the rest will be left behind.' Deaf to our protests, he had made
up his mind."[29]

Refugees from Bosnia-Herzegovina in Croatia. (UNHCR/A. Hollmann)

For many refugees, the violent situations that cause them to flee their home countries are only the beginning of the trauma. The path to refuge may itself be strewn with dangers. During flight, refugee and displaced women and girls have been victimized by pirates, border guards, army and resistance units, male refugees, and others with whom they come in contact. Abduction and rape may be the consequence of seeking asylum for those able to survive the trip.

Piracy attacks in Southeast Asia brought international attention to the physical protection problems faced by women who were the specific focus of many of these attacks. One eyewitness described:

Two of the young and pretty girls were taken to the front of the boat and raped. Everyone heard everything, all of the screams. That is what I remember, the screams. After awhile, the screams stopped, the crying stopped, and there was silence.

You know it was a nightmare and everyone was part of it. You could not close your eyes. You could not close your ears. I still see the faces and hear the cries.[30]

A second boat experienced a similar pattern:

While all the men were confined to the hold of the refugee boat, . . . some, if not all of approximately 15–20 women and young girls who were kept in the cabin of the boat were raped. The youngest of these girls was around 12 years old. Soon afterwards, the pirates set the boat on fire with all the Vietnamese on board. In the ensuing panic, the Vietnamese grabbed buoys, cans, and floats and plunged into the sea. The crews of the pirate boats then used sticks to prevent them from clinging to floating objects. . . . Women and children were the first to perish.[31]

Others reported boat people being forced to choose young girls to be offered to the pirates in exchange for the lives of the rest of the passengers.[32]

An antipiracy campaign funded by the international community to the amount of $2.4 million per year led to the arrest and conviction of pirates in Thailand. It involved cooperation among a number of Thai governmental entities, including the navy, marine police, the harbor department, and the public prosecutor's office. The program includes air and sea patrols, arrests of suspected pirates, and other activities aimed at suppressing piracy. The percentage of boats attacked decreased as a result of these efforts. In response to the increased enforcement measures, however, pirates intensified their attacks killing more people so as to leave no survivors who could testify against them.

While piracy in the South China Sea received much attention, problems during flight existed and continues to exist in other locations as well. For example, a refugee woman interviewed in Djibouti reported:

At age 18, she arrived from the two-week trek through the Danakil desert, physically exhausted, badly dehydrated, and with blistering sores from exposure on her feet and body. But the most terrible part of her ordeal, she points out, was the three days she was held at the border jail and raped repeatedly.[33]

When women are separated from husbands and brothers in the chaos of flight or they are widowed during war, they are especially susceptible to physical abuse and rape. Separation of families often happens during flight. It is sometimes not possible for all members of a family to leave a country together. Even when they leave together, families may be separated en route. Some would-be refugees—for example, Central Americans seeking entry into the United States—utilize the services of smugglers to help them cross borders. "Coyotes," as smugglers of aliens into the United States are called, sometimes separate adults and children at the final entry point. This is done in part to reduce the likelihood that all members of the group will be apprehended. In addition, the presence of children sometimes makes it less likely that the Border Patrol will stop a group because more time is needed in processing these cases.

During the past decade, there has been growing awareness of a new danger to women and children in flight: human traffickers. These criminal operations offer to smuggle would-be asylum seekers to destination countries, particularly in the North, and then keep them in near slaverylike conditions until the smuggling fees are paid. Or, they promise well-paying jobs to susceptible and often frightened women and children, only to entrap them in brothels and other exploitive labor. As wealthier countries have taken measures to deter asylum seekers from reaching their territory, trafficking has only increased and, in many cases, flourished. It is now a multibillion dollar industry, utilizing criminal rings throughout the world. In a particularly brazen case, traffickers were found recruiting Kosovar refugees from camps in Albania and Macedonia during the 1990s.

After Flight

Aycha is 19 and from the Horn of Africa. She arrived in her country of asylum after a two-week trek through the desert. Physically exhausted and suffering from blistering sores she was directed to a refugee settlement but her ordeal was not yet over. A policeman of the neighbouring town raped Aycha after having threatened to have her sent back to her country of origin if she did not comply. The act of rape was subsequently medically confirmed. Charges have been brought against the policeman and Aycha is receiving care and assistance.[34]

Mary Awatch now lives in the third railway car from the front of the train. From the window of the same car, a year ago, she watched a man shoot and kill two of her children during the massacre at Dhein, in southern Sudan. . . . Mary and her remaining children are part of an estimated two million southern Sudanese who have fled their homes due to the civil war that is once again devastating the countryside.[35]

Violence against women and children does not necessarily abate when refugee and displaced women reach the supposed safety of an asylum country or displaced persons camp. Perpetrators of violence against refugee and displaced women and children include not only military personnel from the host and home countries and resistance forces but male refugees and humanitarian aid personnel as well. The abuse may be as flagrant as outright rape and abduction or as subtle as an offer of protection, documents, or assistance in exchange for sexual favors. Unaccompanied women and children are particularly at risk of such sexual and physical abuse.

Revelations about sexual exploitation of refugee children in West Africa brought the issue to international attention in 2002. A study carried out by the UNHCR and Save the Children/U.K. interviewed refugee girls and adolescents in Liberia, Guinea, and Sierra Leone. Noting that the study was not intended to be as rigorous as would be required for a criminal investigation, the report cited numerous examples of sexual exploitation by staff working for international humanitarian organizations. Implicated were employees of UN agencies, including UNHCR, as well as international nongovernmental organizations. The report found "most of the alleged 'exploiters' were male national staff who traded humanitarian commodities and services for sex with girls under 18."[36] Reporting the exploitation by aid workers was not seen as an option. Adolescents in Guinea and Liberia told the study team "If you report one NGO worker you will not only be in trouble with that person, but with the other staff also."[37]

Many factors contribute to the vulnerability of refugee and displaced women and girls to sexual violence and exploitation. Exploitation certainly is related to the absence of alternatives for refugees and displaced persons. When a group is totally dependent on others for economic survival, members of the group are inherently vulnerable to such exploitation. In West Africa, there is extreme dependence on inadequate humanitarian assistance, particularly in the form of food aid. As the study reported, "In every meeting, insufficient ration was raised as a primary factor contributing to sexual exploitation. Food given to the refugee community for thirty days was said to finish within ten days and refugees did not have land to grow their own food to supplement. When the food finished and the family needed more, the immediate option was to get money quickly and buy food."[38] Unfortunately, the potential for this sexual abuse was foreseen at least a decade before. As a UNHCR report noted of Guinea in 1990:

> There is a special need to accelerate the provision of appropriate accommodation to refugee women to ensure their safety and well-being as well as to see that they are not forced into a relationship against their will merely for survival.[39]

Refugee women without proper documentation are particularly susceptible to exploitation and abuse. In many refugee situations, women are not routinely provided documents showing that they are legally in the country.

The male head of household may have been given a document but he is not always present.

In many camps, the physical facilities increase the likelihood of protection problems. Camps are often overcrowded. Unrelated families may be required to share a communal living space. In effect, they are living among strangers, even persons who could be considered traditional enemies. The team examining sexual exploitation in West Africa noted that the "size of the house . . . for larger families in particular . . . is inadequate and affords no privacy. Children are being exposed to sexual activity of adults from an early age."[40]

Closed camps are used in a number of countries where all individuals who enter illegally are subject to detention regardless of age or sex or their application for refugee status. Closed camps are often surrounded by barbed wire, giving the appearance and reality of being prisons with prisonlike lack of regard for individual freedoms. Inhuman surroundings can beget inhumane actions. The author witnessed such conditions in Hong Kong during a visit in 1990. The camps had barracks housing 250 or more people. In the barracks were rows of triple-decker platforms that served as living quarters. A family lived in an area that is about four feet by eight feet. In some cases, families have pieces of cloth to separate their area from their neighbors. In other cases, even this minimal privacy is missing.

> It takes seeing Whitehead and Sek Kong Detention Centres to realize that the warehousing of people belongs to a systematic process of dehumanization, breeding violence and fear. It takes talking to a young woman who tells how, at night, she was raped by three masked men, while holding her child in her arms, to understand how little chance these people have.[41]

More recently, closed detention camps in the United States have given rise to sexual assaults against women asylum seekers. Most notorious has been the Krome Detention Center in Miami, Florida, which at one point was under investigation about allegations of sexual abuse by four agencies of the U.S. Justice Department: the Office of the Inspector General, the Office of Public Integrity, the U.S. Attorneys Office, and the Federal Bureau of Investigation. Pressure from nongovernmental organizations led to removal of women from Krome and their incarceration in other facilities. Unfortunately, similar problems arose in the new location, calling into question the entire detention policy.[42]

What are referred to in Burundi as "regroupment" camps expose internally displaced women and children to particularly horrendous conditions. Regroupment has been a tool of the Burundian government since 1996 when about 300,000 persons, mainly Hutu, were forced into camps, ostensibly for their own protection. Most of these camps closed in 1998 but the last quarter of 1999 saw the creation again of regroupment camps, officially termed "protection sites." Conditions inside the camps were for the most part appalling and some of the camps were inaccessible to humanitarian agencies.[43] Women and children were especially vulnerable when food was short; at food distribution they were often sidelined, sometimes despite efforts of distribution agencies.[44] There were also reports of the rape and sexual abuse of women and young girls in the camps.[45]

There was almost universal condemnation of the camps and extensive calls for their closure. Most were dismantled in the third quarter of 2000 following pressure from Nelson Mandela, the international community, and local organizations.[46] The final pressure came from the rebel groups who made closure of the camps a precondition for joining the peace negotiations. The camp closures occurred within a very short period and with no preparation for the safe return of the regrouped. Some camps were closed very quickly, either because the authorities wanted them emptied as fast as possible but more often because as soon as the camp population was allowed to leave they did, despite the risks and conditions they then faced.

When the regrouped population left the camps, many faced serious risk. Fighting continued or even intensified in many areas to which the regrouped returned. While the international community rightly demanded the closure of the camps, neither they nor the government made adequate preparations for this contingency. The location of most of the formerly regrouped population remains vague. Many appear to have gone home but others are believed to still be living in or near regroupment camps. Still others are likely to have moved to Bujumbura or other parts of the country. No statistics are available on the relative size of each group.[47]

Poor design of camps also contributes to protection problems for women. Although the UNHCR *Guidelines on the Protection of Refugee Women* emphasize the importance of camp layout in ensuring the protection of women, camps do not always follow the recommended design. Moreover, no similar guidelines exist for the design of camps for internally displaced persons. Camps tend to be poorly if at all lit. Among common problems, communal latrines may be at some distance from the living quarters, thereby increasing the potential for attacks on women, especially at night. A UN team investigating allegations of sexual abuse in West Africa found: "Bathing facilities in a number of the camps consist of one building with one side for men and another side for women. The isolation and lack of separate and distinctly placed facilities, which would increase the cost, has caused the facilities to occasionally be the site of sexual violence."[48]

Security is generally inadequate as well. International humanitarian aid staff is often absent from camps, leaving operations to local, national, and refugee staff. Night patrols to ensure greater protection may be absent or infrequent. The responsibility for security generally rests with governments. Yet, government authorities, particularly in poorer countries, usually do not have sufficient resources to fulfill the responsibility. In many cases of internal displacement, in particular, government authorities are hostile to the forced migrants, making them unlikely to protect the security of the women and children. The refugees and displaced themselves may take on the responsibility for patrolling the camps, but their capacities are limited as well.

Traditional mechanisms for protection of the vulnerable may be lost when refugees are forced to live in camps. In particular, the communal support systems for protection of widows, single women, and unaccompanied minors are often no longer present. Spouse and child abuse and abandonment are problems encountered by women and children in refugee and displaced persons situations. Heightened levels of domestic violence are not infrequent where refugees have lived for extended periods of time in the artificial environment of a refugee camp. Psychological strains for husbands and adolescent boys unable to assume normal cultural, social, and economic roles can result in aggressive behavior toward wives, children, and sisters. The enforced idleness, boredom, and despair that permeate many refugee and displaced persons camps are natural breeding grounds for such violence.

Refugee and IDP camps in a number of locations house the civilian families of members of the armed forces. The camps frequently serve as rest and recuperation sites. The men often bring weapons with them into the camps. Proliferation of weapons can compound the protection problems facing refugee women. The camps in then Zaire dominated by the Hutu militias that had committed genocide and continued their armed conflict made this problem highly visible in the mid-1990s. There have been some successful efforts to separate combatants from civilians. In Zambia, for example, a separate camp has been established for former combatants so they do not mix with the refugee population. This strategy is too often followed, however, leading to protection problems for women and children.

Forced recruitment of women and children into the armed forces of resistance groups is a further problem in some countries. They are recruited in some cases as actual soldiers. In other cases, women and children are required to carry ammunition and other supplies. In still other situations, women and children are used to clear mines.

Because refugees and displaced persons are often associated with one or both parties to a civil war, the pressure to provide assistance to the military can be very strong. This is not to say that all such recruitment is forced. In some cases, refugee women may be active and willing participants in their community's struggle. Palestinian women have been active in the intifadas, the uprisings in the Israeli occupied West Bank and Gaza Strip, for example. One of the newly emerging leaders of the Palestinian women's movement said of the first intifada:

> For the first time, we are seeing women participating in various ways in resisting occupation . . . in ways that we think were not possible before the uprising. Women are now very active in neighbourhood committees. Their experience and organizational skills are facilitating these committees' work in providing services to communities. But they now participate as leaders, and not only as service providers.[49]

A Palestinian newsletter further reported:

> The theme underlying the portraits here is one of open defiance of the occupation on the one hand and active defence of community and individual life on the other. We see rural women, women living in refugee camps, and a middle-class woman from a town responding with a striking similarity, despite their different circumstances. Defiance of the occupation and defence of the community: the twin watchwords of women in the Occupied Territories.[50]

Maintaining funding for programs to provide for greater security for refugees and displaced persons has been difficult. During periods of budget cuts, the funds needed to make improvements in camp design may be seen as unnecessary expenditures. Programs funded through special appeals may not be able to maintain a constant level of support. To the extent that the needs of women and children are inadequately integrated into planning and implementation of mainstream policy, or the mainstream programs are facing deep cuts, their physical security will be placed at risk.

When assistance is inadequate, as described above in West Africa but prevalent throughout the world, refugee women may be forced into prostitution to support their families. Prostitution involves primarily single refugee women and girls who are unaccompanied, as well as female heads of household. The causes are generally complex, but key to the decision to become a prostitute is the absence of adequate income. Until alternative income-generating opportunities are made accessible to these women, prostitution will probably remain a too-common occupation. This problem is compounded by minimal assistance programs in many urban locations, particularly where refugees are residing illegally. The reliance on prostitution is particularly acute where men have left their families to fend for themselves. There may be inadequate community resources for helping deserted families and/or inadequate community support for curbing prostitution.

Prosecuting those who attack or exploit women has proven difficult in many situations. The women are often reluctant to talk about the attacks and to go through the emotional and sometimes threatening process of identifying and testifying against the culprits. The perpetrators may be individuals in positions of authority, and those representing the interests of the women are unable or unwilling to bring them to account. Following the revelations of sexual exploitation in West Africa, the United Nations sent out an investigative team to determine if there were grounds for prosecution. The team found: "The [UNHCR/Save the Children U.K.] report of widespread sexual exploitation of refugees has not been confirmed . . . by sufficient evidence for either criminal or disciplinary proceedings."[51] The investigative team concluded, "however, the conditions in the camps and in refugee communities in the three countries in question make refugees vulnerable to sexual and other forms of exploitation and such vulnerability increases if one is a female and young."

A final significant impediment to protection of refugee and displaced women and children is the general insecurity that places humanitarian operations at risk. In modern conflict, civilians have become the targets of armed attack, not just the innocent victims of war. Also targeted are the humanitarian actors that seek to assist and protect civilians. Insecurity is by far the biggest impediment to securing the rights of refugee and displaced women and children, particularly when the displaced are still within their own countries or they remain under the control of military forces in a country of refuge.[52] Insecure conditions impede access to vulnerable populations for delivery of aid, create protection problems for aid workers as well as their clients, and make it impossible to monitor and evaluate the effectiveness of aid operations. Because of attacks on humanitarian aid operations and their consequences, forced migrants too often end up "out of sight and out of mind" of the very humanitarian system that is designed to assist and protect them.

At the start of each complex humanitarian emergency, a professional security assessment should be taken and repeated periodically thereafter. The vulnerabilities of refugee and displaced women and children to attack and exploitation are key issues to cover in such assessments, as are the vulnerabilities of humanitarian aid workers seeking to bring assistance and protection to these populations. The assessments should recommend ways to increase access to and protection of forced migrants and to reduce risk to aid workers.

Peacekeepers can play an important role in securing access to and protecting displaced populations, although their involvement is limited. The decision to intervene with military forces even when loss of life is at risk, and to commit peacekeeping troops to maintain security, is a difficult one that political leaders are generally loathe to make.[53] Nevertheless, humanitarian interventions have occurred with some regularity during the past decade, and peacekeepers are likely to continue to be deployed during humanitarian emergencies. Military forces, such as NATO and the Australian military, have also been called upon to assist with logistics, construction and other aspects of humanitarian aid in such places as Kosovo and East Timor. The peacemaking and peacekeeping forces should have clear mandates to protect civilian populations and humanitarian relief operations in such situations.[54] They should have adequate human and financial resources to fulfill this security mandate, and they should negotiate terms of reference for cooperation with humanitarian agencies. Better training of military forces that are likely to come into contact with civilians, particularly displaced persons, could also help improve security for IDPs, returnees, and other war-affected populations.

At the same time, civilian capabilities to protect forced migrants should be developed. A welcome step is the decision made by the United Nations in January 2002 to provide funding out of the regular budget for staff safety and security activities. UNSECOORD was provided with a core budget to deploy 100 Field Security Officers (FSOs) in crisis areas. Many times the threat to relief operations comes from bandits and criminal elements or loosely organized militias rather than actual military forces. In such situations, civilian policing may be the appropriate way to gain greater security for displaced persons and humanitarian workers. Many agencies maintain rosters of emergency professional personnel who can be called up for short-term assignments. Such a roster of police may be useful in broadening access to the expertise needed for both assessing security problems and identifying and implementing appropriate remedies. Given the scale of insecurity, though, it may be necessary to develop a standing international police force that is explicitly mandated to protect humanitarian operations. The UNSECOORD FSOs may form the core of such a group.

Humanitarian organizations must also look to their own programs to reduce the vulnerability of forced migrants to attacks, abuses, and exploitation. As described above, the reports of sexual exploitation of refugees and displaced children in West Africa highlighted problems that have long been known or suspected. Dependency on humanitarian aid creates vulnerability to exploitation by unscrupulous officials, military, police, and aid workers. If the aid is insufficient, and no legitimate economic opportunities are available, women and children will be forced to take other measures, including prostitution, in order to feed themselves and their families. These problems arise in all settings, affecting refugees and displaced persons in camps and spontaneously settled in rural and urban areas.

To summarize, the steps that can be taken to improve the physical protection of refugee and displaced women include:

- Place international staff in border areas that refugee women must cross in order to enter countries of asylum as well as in reception centers, refugee camps, and settlements.
- Improve the design of refugee and displaced persons camps to promote greater physical security. Special measures that should be implemented include security patrols, special accommodations if needed for single women, women heads of households and unaccompanied minors, improved lighting, and physical barriers to the access of armed persons to camps.
- Provide gender-sensitive training for host country border guards, police, military units, and others who come into contact with refugee and displaced persons.
- Ensure greater participation of refugee and displaced women in decisions affecting their security. Among the issues requiring greater input from the women are mechanisms to improve the reporting of physical and sexual protection problems.
- Employ female protection officers and social and community workers to identify and provide remedies for women and children who are victims of physical violence and sexual abuse.
- Ensure that refugee and displaced women are not forced to stay for protracted periods of time in closed refugee camps or detention centers where they are likely to be the victims of family and intracommunal violence.
- Establish effective mechanisms for law enforcement to ensure that abusers are identified and prosecuted for their offenses.
- Address protection concerns particular to refugee and displaced women in all sectors of refugee programs.

CONCLUSION

The protection of refugee and displaced women should be of the highest priority to the international community. As seen from this discussion, protection is a concept that encompasses many aspects of a refugee's life from physical safety to legal rights. A key condition of effective protection is access to the assistance needed to survive within a refugee and displaced persons context. The next chapter spells out in greater detail the various assistance needs of the uprooted women and their dependents.

NOTES

Full citations can be found in the select bibliography.

1. UNHCR, *UNHCR and Refugee Women: International Protection* (Geneva: UNHCR, 1985).
2. Amnesty International, "Nigeria: Condemnation of the Death Penalty. Concerns on the Implementation of New Sharia-Based Penal Codes," Updated March 26, 2003. Available at www.amnesty.org.au/women/action-letter09.html.
3. BBC News, "Pakistan Court Rules on Adultery," August 21, 2002. Available at news.bbc.co.uk/2/low/south_asia/2208171.stm.
4. Elizabeth Ferris, *Refugee Women and Violence* (Geneva: World Council of Churches, 1990), 2.
5. Human Rights Watch, "Human Rights Watch Applauds Rwanda Rape Verdict: Sets International Precedent for Punishing Sexual Violence as a War Crime," September 2, 1998. Available at www.hrw.org/press98/sept/rrape902.htm.
6. Rome Statute, A/CONF.183/9 of July 17, 1998 and corrected by procès-verbaux of November 10, 1998; July 12, 1999; November 30, 1999; May 8, 2000; January 17, 2001; and January 16, 2002.
7. UNHCR, *Note on Refugee Women and International Protection* (Geneva: UNHCR, 1990), 5.
8. UNHCR, "Guidelines on International Protection: Gender-Related Persecution within the Context of Article 1A(2) of the 1951 Convention and/or Its 1967 Protocol Relating to the Status of Refugees," (May 7, 2002).
9. Among the governments issuing guidelines are Australia, Canada, Ireland, the Netherlands, Norway, South Africa, Sweden, the United Kingdom, and the United States.
10. Demirkaya v SSHD (CA) [1999] INLR 441, [1999] Imm AR 498.
11. Fatin v INS 12F. 3d 1233 (3rd Cir. 1993).
12. U.K. Immigration Appellate Authority, "Asylum Gender Guidelines," November 2000. Available at www.iaa.gov.uk/general_info/iaa_gender.htm.
13. U.K. Immigration Appellate Authority, "Asylum Gender Guidelines."
14. Inger Agger, "Sexual Torture of Political Prisoners: An Overview," *Journal of Traumatic Stress* 2, no. 3 (1989).
15. Islam v SSHD; R v IAT ex parte Shah (HL) [1999] INLR 144, [1999] Imm AR 283.
16. Ahmed 1993 FCJ 718 Canada FCA 1993.

17. UNHCR, "Guidelines on International Protection: 'Membership of a Particular Social Group' Within the Context of Article 1A(2) of the 1951 Convention and/or Its 1967 Protocol Relating to the Status of Refugees," (May 7, 2002).

18. Immigration and Refugee Board, "Women Refugee Claimants Fearing Gender-Related Persecution," updated November 13, 1996.

19. U.K. Immigration Appellate Authority, "Asylum Gender Guidelines."

20. Guy Goodwin-Gill, *The Refugee in International Law* (Oxford: Oxford University Press, 1996), 49.

21. Roberta Cohen and Francis Deng, 1998, both in *Rights Have No Borders*, ed. W. Davies.

22. Article 17, Protocol II of 1949 Geneva Conventions.

23. Susan Forbes Martin, *Handbook for Implementing the Guiding Principles on Internal Displacement* (New York: UN Office for the Coordination of Humanitarian Affairs, 1999).

24. African Training and Research Centre for Women, *Refugee and Displaced Women in Independent African States* (Addis Ababa: Economic Commission for Africa, 1986), 22.

25. UNHCR Global Consultations on International Protection, "Practical Aspects of Physical and Legal Protection with Regard to Registration," EC/GC/01/6, February 19, 2001. Available at www.unhcr.ch/prexcom/globalcon.htm.

26. UNHCR, "UNHCR and Refugee Women: International Protection."

27. Women's Commission for Refugee Women and Children, *If Not Now, When? Addressing Gender-Based Violence in Refugee, Internally Displaced, and Post-Conflict Settings. A Global Overview* (New York: Women's Commission on Refugee Women and Children, 2002).

28. Julie Mertus et al., *The Suitcase*, 66.

29. Annick Roulet-Billard, "First Person Feminine," *Refugees* 70 (1989): 25.

30. Tenhula, *Voices from Southeast Asia*, 69.

31. UNHCR, "A Tale of Horror" *Refugees* 65 (1989): 25.

32. Dao Tu Khuong, "Victims of Violence in the South China Sea," in *Refugees: The Trauma of Exile*, ed. Diana Miserez (Dordrecht: Martinus Nijhoff, 1988), 24.

33. Roberta Aitchison, "Reluctant Witnesses," *Cultural Survival Quarterly* 8, no. 2 (Summer 1984): 26.

34. UNHCR, *UNHCR and Refugee Women: International Protection* (Geneva: UNHCR, 1985).

35. Lance Clark, "Internal Refugees: The Hidden Half," in *World Refugee Survey—1988 in Review* (Washington, D.C.: U.S. Committee for Refugees, 1989).

36. UNHCR and Save the Children/U.K., *Note for Implementing and Operational Partners on Sexual Violence and Exploitation of Refugee Children in West Africa* (released February 2002), 4

37. UNHCR and Save the Children/U.K., *Note* 5.

38. UNHCR and Save the Children/U.K., *Note* 8.

39. UNHCR Technical Support Service, *Guinea: An Assessment of the Situation of Liberian Refugee Women and Children* (Geneva: UNHCR, 1990), 2.

40. UNHCR Technical Support Service, *Guinea* 9.

41. Women's Commission for Refugee Women and Children, *Report of Delegation to Hong Kong, January 5–12, 1990* (New York: International Rescue Committee, 1990).

42. See Women's Commission for Refugee Women and Children, *Behind Locked Doors: Abuse of Refugee Women at the Krome Detention Center*, report of an investigation into abuses of asylum seekers detained by the Immigration and Naturalization Service at the Krome Detention Center, Miami, October 2000; and *Innocents in Jail: INS Moves Refugee Women from Krome to Turner Guilford Knight Correctional Center, Miami*, report of investigation into abuses of women asylum seekers detained by the Immigration and Naturalization Service at the TGK Correctional Center, Miami, July 2001.

43. Refugees International, "Burundian Regroupment Camps: A Man-Made Humanitarian Emergency, an Impediment to Peace," January 20, 2000, and "Conditions in Burundian Camps Rapidly Deteriorating," March 1, 2000; Human Rights Watch, *Emptying the Hills, Regroupment in Burundi* (New York: Human Rights Watch, June 2000). Available at www.hrw.org/reports/2000/burundi2/; Amnesty International, "Medical Letter Writing Action, Conditions in 'Regroupment' Camps, Burundi," December 22, 1999, AI Index: AFR 16/036/99.

44. Women's Commission for Refugee Women and Children, *Out of Sight, Out of Mind: Conflict and Displacement in Burundi* (New York: Women's Commission for Refugee Women and Children, October 2000). I led the delegation that produced this report. Available at www.womenscommission.org/reports/index.html.

45. Human Rights Watch, *Emptying the Hills*, 18–20.

46. See, for example, "Forced Relocation in Burundi, Report of the Representative of the Secretary-General on Internally Displaced Persons," UNHCHR, Doc. E/CN.4/2001/5/Add.1 (March 5, 2000). Available at 193.194.138.190/Huridocda/Huridoca.nsf/TestFrame/aff2c994e03ca244c12569d000471a5d?Opendocument.

47. Women's Commission, *Out of Sight, Out of Mind*.

48. United Nations General Assembly, "Investigation into Sexual Exploitation of Refugees by Aid Workers in West Africa: Report of the Secretary-General on the Activities of the Office of Internal Oversight Services," A/57/465 Fifty-seventh Session, Agenda item 122, October 11, 2002.

49. Rita Giacaman, "Palestinian Women in the Uprising: From Followers to Leaders," *Journal of Refugee Studies* 2, no. 1 (1989): 142.

50. Giacaman, "Palestinian Women."

51. United Nations, "Investigation into Sexual Exploitation of Refugees."

52. This conclusion is based largely on the author's participation in a three-year collaborative project on barriers to effective assistance and protection for forced migrants. The study team conducted field visits in Burundi, Sri Lanka, Colombia, East Timor, and Georgia. Consistently, the case studies revealed insecurity to be the principal barrier to assistance and protection, particularly when humanitarian aid operations were the target of military activities. Preliminary findings were presented at the biannual meeting of the International Association for the Study of Forced Migration, Chiang Mai, Thailand, 2003.

53. This section is based on the author's own participation in meetings called by the National Security Council to discuss military intervention in Kosovo and ways to deal with the resulting humanitarian response to forced migration.

54. The study on sexual exploitation in West Africa reported violations by peace-keepers as well as humanitarian staff. In such places as Bosnia and Kosovo, human trafficking for the sex trade has increased along with the presence of peacekeeping staff, in part because the generally young male members of the peacekeeping forces frequent brothels.

Refugees and Internally Displaced Persons in Liberia—Water Supply. (UNHCR/L. Taylor)

4

Assistance: Friend or Foe?

Life in Tendelti is unimaginably harsh. The water is nauseously turbid and smelly. The food is insubstantial and unappetizing. The straw hovels they live in are little more than raffia mats propped up by sticks, no protection against the torrential rainstorms which come every other day. But the women of Tendelti are finding ways to live there with the 4,000 children under the age of seven.[1]

Many of the world's refugees and internally displaced persons (IDPs) are totally dependent on international assistance for their basic needs including food, shelter, water, and health care. For new arrivals, this situation is not surprising. Refugees and displaced persons fleeing their homes usually cannot bring material resources with them. The clothing on their backs and perhaps a small bundle of belongings are often all that they have been able to bring with them. They may arrive in poor health, malnourished, and/or disabled, having experienced famine in their countries of origin and long treks through hazardous terrain.

That large numbers of refugees and displaced persons continue to be dependent on international assistance long after their original flight is more disturbing. In many host countries, refugees remain in care-and-maintenance camps for years, unable to return to home communities because of continued conflict and instability but denied opportunities to work or access to training or income-producing activities. The refugees must rely on food rations, clothing, and shelter as provided by international donors. Of a bare subsistence nature even at the best of times, during periods of financial strain, the assistance package is often inadequate to meet even the basic nutritional needs of the population. Further, there is too little coordination among the various sections of assistance—health, education, skills training, for example—to better facilitate independence.

Refugee and displaced women are triply affected by this international assistance system. As the principal beneficiaries of assistance, they and their children suffer from the inadequacies in the assistance package. Unable to obtain employment and often denied participation in training or income generation programs, they are unable to provide for their families without the international assistance. With it, they may still be vulnerable, as seen in the previous chapter, to sexual abuse and exploitation. And, finally, they are not adequately consulted about the programs in place nor are they permitted to participate actively in the implementation of projects ostensibly designed to assist them.

This chapter presents an overview of the assistance issues encountered by refugee and displaced women, using the information gleaned from the author's field visits to refugee and displaced persons camps and the reports of individuals and groups working with refugee women.

ACCESS TO FOOD, WATER, AND NONFOOD ITEMS

A principal cause of mortality in humanitarian emergencies is malnutrition. Lack of food kills on its own and is a major contributor to death from a number of diseases. Malnourished people are more susceptible to disease and are more difficult to cure of illnesses. Malnourished women who are pregnant or lactating are unable to provide sufficient nutrients to their children to enable them to survive. In addition to food problems, poor sanitation and contaminated water supplies contribute to high death rates in many refugee situations. A recent retrospective study of death rates in humanitarian emergencies found "Camps with less water per person and high rates of diarrhea had higher child (under five years of age) death rates."[2] People denied such basic items as shelter, clothing, and cooking utensils are also at higher risk of disease.

According to the UNHCR *Handbook for Emergencies*, "a minimum requirement of 2,100 kcal per person per day is used as the planning figure for a developing country population at the beginning of an emergency."[3] These requirements are consistent with the Sphere Project standards, an effort by nongovernmental organizations (NGOs) to set minimum standards for humanitarian emergency operations.[4] The diet must satisfy protein and basic vitamin requirements and must pay particular attention to locally prevalent nutritional deficiencies. A typical daily ration would be built around a staple food (such as cereal), an energy-rich food (such as oil), and a protein-rich food (for example, beans).[5]

Two types of ration distribution are used. The preferred method is dry ration distribution where the refugees take the ration home and prepare the food as they wish. This method requires distribution of cooking pots, fuel, and utensils as well. The second is cooked food distribution where central kitchens are established and the refugees collect already prepared meals.

While the cooked food distribution can be culturally more problematic, it is used under emergency circumstances when individual cooking facilities and equipment are not available. Communal cooking continues over the longer term in some camps. In some cases, this process serves to undermine family structures and roles since it changes traditional responsibilities for provision and preparation of food. With full participation of women in decisions on communal cooking, however, it can serve the purpose of increasing community cohesion:

> Two large kitchens served the entire camp, and nearly all of the women participated in the food preparation and distribution. They served on teams which rotated on a daily basis. The community kitchen promoted community living and ensured equal access to a good diet for all. Representatives, chosen from teams, participated in the menu planning and evaluation sessions. These sessions took into consideration such concerns as: the customs and preferences of the people, special dietary needs, seasonal availability of local as well as home-grown fruits and vegetables, nutritional standards, and budgetary constraints. Two of the women were also responsible for the twice-weekly purchasing of perishable foods.
>
> The aim was to provide a well-balanced diet that was acceptable to the people, adaptable to special needs (the elderly, pregnant and lactating women, children and the infirm) and yet simple enough to be transferable to future living situations outside the camp. For this reason, expensive items such as meat, fish and chicken were included in the diet only in limited amounts.[6]

Equal access to food and nonfood items is a key issue for refugee and displaced women and children. Decisions about food distribution are generally made by international organizations and host countries, often in consultation with the refugee leaders of the camps. Refugee leadership structures, particularly at the height of emergencies, often exclude women. Yet, male leaders may have little understanding of the needs and circumstances of those who cook the food or feed their families—the women. As a result, the food distribution procedures and contents may be inappropriate. Food that is inconsistent with the dietary traditions of the refugees and displaced persons may be provided. Or, food may be offered that requires preparation that cannot be readily accomplished in the camp setting. These problems are further compounded by cultural practices among some refugee and displaced populations that require that men be fed first. Where supplies are limited, women and children may not receive adequate food.

During the past decade, there has been increased recognition that women must be involved early in the process in the design of food distribution systems as well as in the actual delivery of the food. The UNHCR *Guidelines on the Protection of Refugee Women* recommend that UNHCR staff "consult with refugee women regarding all decisions about food and other distribution [and] designate refugee women as the initial point of contact for emergency and longer-term food distribution."[7] World Food Program (WFP) policies say that women should control the family food aid entitlement in 80 percent of WFP food distributions. The WFP guidelines also state that women should take a lead role in local decision-making committees on food aid management as well as the management of assets created through food-for-work programs.

These guidelines recognize that male-dominated food distribution is often at clear odds with traditional patterns in which women play a lead role in food production. The World Bank reports that 70 percent of the food grown in developing countries is produced by women. Although the pattern differs somewhat by region, women in developing countries are also typically involved in animal husbandry, activities aimed at storing food, selling and exchanging produce, and the preparation and cooking of food. In Africa, women are often the sole cultivators whereas in Asia, joint cultivation by spouses is more typical. In Latin America, women tend to take over cultivation when their husbands seek employment in the cities to supplement agricultural work.[8]

The guidelines also recognize that food distributed through male networks has been diverted to resistance forces or for sale on the black market, with women and children suffering as a result. Food has also been used as a weapon by both government and resistance forces, which have blocked distribution to civilian populations, particularly displaced persons. In still other cases, male distributors of food and other items have required sexual favors in exchange for the assistance goods, as discussed above.

Distribution of food directly to women can reduce some of these problems. Female distribution systems were tested during the 1980s in the camps along the Thai-Cambodian border with good success. The UN Border Relief Operation (UNBRO) provided rations to women and girls over the age of eight for redistribution or sale, as needed, to cover the needs of the camps. This policy succeeded in reducing the diversion of food to the military. It required some changes over time, however, because families with few or no girls tended to be disadvantaged in comparison with those with a larger number of female members.

Distributing food directly to women may place them at risk if steps are not taken to protect them during and after collection. As a focus group assembled in February 2000 by the World Food Program in southern Sudan pointed out, "women beneficiaries face risks when attending a distribution: the risk of having their food aid looted by non-targeted members of the community who have turned up at the distribution site; and the risk of being left with little food after redistribution to relatives and neighbours." On the other hand, the group did not feel that violence against women at distribution points was a serious, recurrent problem though the members recognized it could be a serious threat. The group concluded that "men should not be given food aid (unless they are widowers) since women have traditional responsibility for food aid management within the household."[9]

Too often, food rations are inadequate to meet the needs of the population even when there is no diversion of aid. Inadequacies in funding are largely to blame. This problem is a persistent one. In 1992, this book explained the problem in the following way: "WFP is facing major shortfalls in food supplies at the same time that a budgetary crisis at UNHCR impedes its ability to cushion ration cuts by purchasing additional food. The basic ration in a number of locations has been cut both in calories and in content. As a result, outbreaks of such diseases as scurvy and pellagra have been reported in Ethiopia, Angola, Malawi, Swaziland, and Zimbabwe. Increases in childhood malnutrition have been reported in these countries as well as Hong Kong, Mexico, and Thailand." A decade later, the U.S. Committee for Refugees (USCR) writes: "Programs to assist and protect refugees worldwide currently face a financial crisis. Funding by donor nations for international refugee programs has been seriously inadequate during 2002, triggering major assistance cutbacks in refugee camps around the world." Among the casualties of the financial crisis, according to USCR: "Funding constraints forced cutbacks in food deliveries to 80,000 refugees from Western Sahara living in arid camps where farming was impossible (Algeria); in a region with more than 800,000 refugees, budget problems caused relief workers to cut refugees' food rations (Horn of Africa); budget problems forced a 25 percent cut in food rations for up to 80,000 Sudanese refugees (Kenya); and funding shortfalls forced a 50 percent cut in food rations for 35,000 refugees from Congo-Kinshasa, resulting in higher malnutrition rates (Zambia)."[10]

Among adults, women are particularly susceptible to problems arising from inadequacies in the basic ration. Women are affected by deficiencies in iron, calcium, iodine, and vitamin C. Pregnant women and lactating mothers are very much at risk. For example, pregnant women who are anemic run the risk of fatal hemorrhaging during childbirth. Supplemental feeding programs may be essential to maintain even a modicum of good health for these women and their children.

The limited composition of the basic food ration is also problematic. The Sphere Project recognizes: "Some of the food rations used currently for populations that are fully dependent on food aid may not be sufficient to meet requirements (particularly riboflavin [vitamin B2], niacin [vitamin B3], vitamin C, iron and folic acid)."[11] The ration does not generally include meat, fish, vegetables, fruit, and other foods needed for a balanced diet. Generally, beneficiaries of food aid are expected to barter the ration for other food items, or it is expected that they will grow vegetables, raise livestock, or work for currency and buy food. Without access to such opportunities, however, refugee and displaced women may find themselves with few options if they want to feed themselves and their families. A recent assessment of compliance with the UNHCR *Guidelines on the Protection of Refugee Women* found: "The assessment team learned of many instances of women in Zambian camps exchanging sex for fish. Because the refugee diet is mainly comprised of grains and oil, fish—although scarce—is much desired. In many cases, the women complied but never received the fish. In a number of sites, women described others who contracted sexually transmitted diseases by exchanging sexual favors for otherwise unavailable food and non-food items."[12]

Clean water is another essential need. Women in refugee and displaced persons camps, like many other women in developing countries, spend a great deal of time in water collection. Containers that are too heavy or pumps that are inconveniently located can intensify this effort. When clean water is not available, children, in particular, run the risk of life-threatening diarrheal diseases. The absence of clean water in urban settings is particularly problematic, especially when populations have been dependent on water distribution systems that are destroyed during conflict. During the 2003 Iraq War, most of the water systems in Baghdad and other Iraqi cities were destroyed, or could not work because of destruction of the electrical systems, leaving civilian populations with no access to clean water. A high priority of the humanitarian aid system was the delivery of water and rebuilding of the water systems.

Collection of fuel for cooking and heating is also a task for which women are generally responsible. In a refugee or displaced persons context, however, efforts to find firewood can be not only time-consuming (if located at some distance from the camps) but dangerous (if located in mine-infested areas or the site of conflict). In the Dadaab refugee camps in Kenya, Somali women were frequently attacked by bandits as they traveled further and further from the camps to gather firewood. During a visit to the camps in 1996, this author asked refugee women why the men did not collect the firewood. They responded: "women are raped if they leave the camp; the men are killed." The assessment of the UNHCR *Guidelines* found women collecting firewood at risk in Ethiopia, and potentially in Zambia: "In both cases, women who gather firewood are at risk of physical harm—not primarily due to rape as in the well-documented Dadaab camp case—but because of local hostility to refugees who are depleting scarce resources."[13] Lack of funding is the major barrier to solving this problem, as it is in many others. The assessment goes on to explain: "Possible alternatives to firewood were considered too expensive in Ethiopia, but are being considered in a preliminary way in Zambia."[14]

A further persistent problem is the distribution of sanitary materials. Since 1996, UNHCR has required all field programs to include sanitary materials in regular budgets. A survey of fifty-two UNHCR offices found low compliance, however.[15] The unavailability of these materials is not just an inconvenience to refugee women and adolescents. Rather, it is a major impediment to their full participation in the life of the camp society: "In both Ethiopia and Zambia girls stayed away from school and sometimes remaining in their houses because they had nothing decent to wear during monthly menstruation."[16]

HEALTH CARE

The access of refugee and displaced women and children to health care services is important both to their own health and to the welfare of the broader community. Women typically bear responsibility for all family chores, fuel gathering, water collection, childcare, and cooking. Should a woman die or become incapacitated, she is unable to perform these tasks, thereby putting her family at risk. Women are also the prime providers of health care to other family members. Thus, the health of other members of the family will be directly related to a mother's knowledge or interest in promoting a healthy environment and taking preventive actions against disease.

Health Problems of Refugee and Displaced Women

The health problems refugee and displaced women and children face are similar to those of other women and children in developing countries, but many of them are compounded by the refugee experience. Nutritional problems have been discussed. Refugee women can suffer from physical disabilities resulting from their refugee experience. They may be the victims of mine explosions, for example. Loss of limbs is not uncommon both in flight and during stays in camps.

Once the emergency phase is over, a leading cause of death among refugee and displaced women of childbearing age is complications from pregnancies. Lack of training of midwives and traditional birth attendants (TBA), septic abortions, unsanitary conditions during birth, septic instruments, poor lighting during deliveries, and frequency of pregnancies all lead to difficulties.

The Sphere Project recommends: "Neo-natal and maternal morbidity and mortality should be prevented by: establishing ante-natal services for preparing to handle obstetric emergencies; making available and distributing clean delivery kits; ensuring that UNICEF midwife TBA kits or the UNFPA reproductive health emergency kits are available at health centres."[17]

Problems are compounded by high birthrates in many refugee and displaced persons camps, rates that sometimes exceed traditional birthrates prior to flight. Spiraling birthrates result from a variety of factors—for example, means of birth control may not be available or usable in the refugee setting, refugee groups that have lost significant numbers of children may want to rebuild their population, and cultural and social values may support large families.

Refugee and displaced women are particularly susceptible to water-borne diseases. They are generally responsible for collecting and storing water. Contaminated water causes such illnesses as typhoid, cholera, dysentery, and infectious hepatitis. In addition, women are at risk of being infected with diseases that are carried by insects that breed or bite near water: for example, sleeping sickness, malaria, yellow fever, and river blindness. Moreover, women are also at risk of infection with diseases transmitted through contact with water, such as worms and schistosomiasis.

Measles and other diseases that can be prevented through immunizations are a too-frequent cause of death in refugee and displaced persons camps. These illnesses particularly affect children. As explained by the Sphere Project, "Measles is one of the most contagious and lethal viruses known. Crowded emergency settings and unexpected population movements provide an ideal environment for the rapid and intense transmission of this virus, which can result in high levels of morbidity and mortality, especially among young children."[18]

During the past decade, great strides have been made to ensure vaccination of children as soon as possible. The Sphere Standards emphasize "In disaster-affected populations, all children 6 months to 12 years old receive a dose of measles vaccine and an appropriate dose of vitamin A as soon as possible."[19]

Health complications also arise from female circumcision, also known as female genital mutilation (FGM), a practice in some parts of Africa and the Middle East that carries over into refugee and displaced persons camps. Problems include: infections due to instruments that are not sterile, damage to adjacent organs, obstructed menstrual flow, painful intercourse, severe blood loss, and obstetric complications.[20]

Health workers are often insufficiently knowledgeable about the practice and consequences of female circumcision. They need training to recognize and treat symptoms. In addition, educational efforts are needed to inform the refugees and displaced persons about the health hazards of female circumcision. Traditional birth attendants should be a principal target of these efforts. They should also be informed of educational campaigns used in other places to reduce the incidence of female circumcision. Refugee women may not be aware that progress has been made in eliminating this practice. That such programs can be effective is found in the assessment of the UNHCR *Guidelines*: "In the camps visited in Ethiopia FGM exists among a small group of Sudanese; it is more prevalent among the Somali refugees. Girls' education helps to reduce the practice and in at least one camp refugee boys have proven to be good advocates against FGM. Prior to the team visit, UNHCR in Ethiopia had reduced the incidence of FGM by means of regular workshops and training for women. UNHCR facilitated training of the practitioners in the Dadaab complex of camps in Kenya in the mid-1990s about the deleterious health effects of FGM, which resulted in the trainees' decision to reduce the invasiveness of the procedure."[21]

In addition to physical health problems, some refugee and displaced women suffer from mental health problems. Becoming a refugee involves many dislocations and abrupt changes in life. At a minimum, refugee and displaced women face emotional problems and difficulties in adjustment resulting from loss of family and community support.

More serious mental health problems are not uncommon, arising from torture and sexual abuse prior or after flight. As we have seen in the chapter on protection issues, rape and abduction are to be found in many refugee situations. Depression and post-traumatic stress disorder often follow such experiences. Common symptoms experienced by survivors of traumatic events include anxiety, intrusive thoughts, disassociation or psychic numbing, hyperalterness, and sleeping and eating disorders. The most serious mental health problems of refugees may manifest themselves in severe depressive behavior, self-destructive behavior, violent or disruptive behavior, alcohol or drug abuse, and a high degree of psychosomatic illness.[22]

As one Afghan physician stated:

> Many women fall victim to depression or neurasthenia as a result of their loneliness and uprooting from their homes. Some come to see me only in order to obtain moral support and have someone with whom they can talk. They are happy to find a doctor who, like themselves is a woman, and who speaks their language.[23]

As discussed in greater length later, there has been a growth in psychosocial programs, gender and sexual violence programs, and reproductive health care programs in recent years. All of these have roles to play in addressing the physical and mental health ramifications of this trauma.

Access to Services

In contrast to other sectors, refugees are sometimes advantaged relative to their neighboring populations in access to health care services. Special programs may be implemented in refugee camps; expatriate physicians and nurses offer their services. Yet, access to health care is not universal in humanitarian emergencies producing mass relocations of people. Groups that often find it difficult to gain access include internally displaced persons, who may be located in areas that are inaccessible or dangerous; returnees, who may be returning to areas with no remaining health infrastructure; spontaneously settled refugees who are outside of formal camp settings and are reliant on host country facilities (to the extent they can legally use these services); and women and children, as described below.

Impediments to health care for refugee and displaced women and children often involve logistical matters. Concerns about security impede access. In some areas, women are reluctant to go to clinics because they must cross insecure areas to get there. In one camp in Hong Kong, visited by the author, passes to the clinic were issued by camp leaders who asked for bribes or sexual favors. Inconvenient clinic hours may prevent women from coming for health services or bringing their children. Other time-consuming responsibilities limit women's flexibility. Also, clinics may be too distant from home.

Inappropriate design of health programs is another impediment to their effective utilization by refugee and displaced women and children. Although an emphasis on preventive programming is supposed to dominate health care systems, many programs are still primarily focused on curative services. In many situations, men are the primary users of in-patient facilities. Some hospital beds are used almost exclusively by soldiers who have returned to their families in refugee and displaced persons camps because they have been wounded or suffer from such diseases as malaria. While this fact presents a set of issues that are outside the scope of this book, it is significant for this purpose because such use of health care services is often at the expense of preventive efforts that would improve the health status of women and children.

Inappropriate or inaccessible health services can be obstacles to good health among refugee and displaced women and their families. The absence of female health practitioners has been one of the principal barriers to health care, particularly where cultural values prevent a woman from being seen by a man who is not a member of her immediate family. This has been a recurrent problem that the international community has not yet solved. During the 1980s, studies attributed underutilization of health services by Afghan refugee women in Pakistan and Cambodian women along the Thai-Cambodian border to reluctance to be treated by male health personnel. In 2002, the assessment of

UNHCR's *Guidelines* found: "There were few or no women health workers in some locations. Some women expressed reluctance to seek help from male doctors. The complete absence of women health workers in such situations should be addressed urgently by UNHCR, particularly since this has come up in evaluations over the past decade. In many—if not most—of these situations, the presence of women health care workers would likely have resulted in thousands of lives saved."[24]

There is also a systematic failure to utilize the existing networks of female health practitioners in refugee communities. A number of programs have trained refugee men to serve as medics but then find that the trained personnel leave the camps. Some seek resettlement abroad; others are conscripted to serve as medics in military forces. By contrast, women health workers tend to be not only more appropriate practitioners but also more stable members of the community. As an assessment of one program along the Thai-Cambodian border found:

> The [nongovernmental organization] had been working in the refugee camp . . . for five years, trying to build up a refugee health care system. The main effort was training medics as primary health care providers. But each time a new crop of medics was trained, they disappeared.
>
> At the same time, the Khmer Women's Association (KWA) was training women in literacy throughout the camp. The literacy program included lessons on hygiene and nutrition. Each zone of the camp had a women's association office. The older women were in charge of the system. They represented the most stable elements of the camp population, having responsibility for their families, while their husbands were present in the camp only intermittently for "rest and recuperation."
>
> The NGO focused on immediate medical needs and provided excellent curative care. By training Khmer medics, the agency's staff transferred skills and information to the refugee population, but neglected the social network that would have promoted health throughout the camp. It missed the opportunity to work with the KWA, strengthening their capacities to build a stable curative and preventive health system in the control of the refugees themselves.[25]

Recruitment of women to become health workers is thus essential to the operation of health services. Special efforts must be made to identify women within the uprooted community, including traditional birth attendants, who have the trust and confidence of other refugee and displaced women. Agencies that place high value on English skills and literacy in their local workers may need to change their criteria for recruitment of health workers if insufficient numbers of refugee and displaced women fit them. They may also need to redesign their training programs to include an emphasis on the development of literacy skills. Further, they may need to develop mechanisms for convincing male leaders that women should become health workers, particularly where there are cultural constraints on women taking employment outside of the home. Recruitment of women as expatriate and host country staff will also need to be intensified, particularly in those posts involving supervision of refugee women staff and clinical services for women.

Model Health Programs

A bright spot in this situation is the growth, during the past decade, in reproductive health services aimed at refugee and displaced women and girls as well as programs to address sexual and gender-based violence and psychosocial needs. Prior to recent years, health services for refugees and displaced persons too often overlooked female-specific needs. For example, gynecological services were usually inadequate. Serious problems, such as infections and cervical cancer, went all but undetected. Counseling regarding sexually transmitted diseases was absent. Few if any programs focused on the needs of adolescent girls even though early marriages and pregnancies are a reported cause of poor health. Access to family planning information and devices was limited in most refugee camps even where it was available to women in the host country (Pakistan, for example). The assessment of UNHCR's *Guidelines* concluded "that UNHCR and its partners have made important strides in providing reproductive health services. In contrast to a decade ago, when such services were rare, they are presently an integral part of health care delivery programs in some places."[26]

During the 1990s, attention began to grow about the dangers to the reproductive health of refugee and displaced women from the absence of appropriate health services. The 1991 UNHCR *Guidelines on the Protection of Refugee Women* recommended "high priority to the provision of primary health care, including maternal and child health services, gynecological services, birthing care, counseling regarding sexually transmitted diseases, family planning programs, and health education regarding public health and harmful practices such as female circumcision."[27] They emphasized that special attention should be given to adolescent children. The 1994 Plan of Action of the International Conference on Population and Development (referred to as the Cairo Conference) recognized the special reproductive health needs of refugees and displaced persons. Following the conference, the Interagency Working Group on Refugee Reproductive Health (IAWG) was formed by representatives of UN agencies, NGOs, and governments. The IAWG produced a field manual that outlined a "Minimum Initial Service Package (MISP)," subsequently included in the Sphere Project standards, "designed to prevent and manage the consequences of sexual violence, reduce HIV transmission, prevent excess neonatal and maternal morbidity and mortality, and plan for the provision of comprehensive reproductive health services." Several NGOs also came together as the Reproductive Health for Refugees Consortium to offer actual services for refugee and displaced women and girls.

Safe motherhood is an essential component of the MISP. In the acute stage of a humanitarian emergency, neonatal and maternal morbidity and mortality can be reduced by providing clean delivery kits to promote clean home deliveries, providing midwife delivery kits to facilitate clean and safe deliveries in health facilities, and initiating the establishment of a referral system to manage obstetric emergencies. Once conditions have become more stable, comprehensive services for antenatal, delivery, and postpartum care should be established.[28] Also needing attention are postabortion complications for those suffering the complications of spontaneous and unsafe abortion. To the extent possible, the needs of both the refugee and displaced and the local population should be addressed. This is particularly important because most refugees and internally displaced persons are in countries with high maternal and infant mortality rates.

Family planning services are a second priority in reproductive health services. The IAWG emphasizes: "Refugee women and men should be involved in all aspects of family planning programs; and the programs should be conducted with full respect for the various religious and ethical values and cultural backgrounds within the refugee community."[29] From the beginning of an emergency, relief organizations should be able to respond to the need for contraception, particularly the distribution of condoms. Providing a full range of family planning services may require more stable conditions. A range of contraceptives should be provided, as well as assessment of needs, counseling and information about methods, and follow-up care to ensure continuity of services. Providers must have the technical skills to offer the methods safely, and they must have an adequate logistics system to ensure continuity of supplies.

Prevention and treatment of sexually transmitted diseases (STDs) is particularly important in humanitarian emergencies involving mass movements of people. As the field manual explains:

> STDs, including HIV/AIDS, spread fastest where there is poverty, powerlessness and social instability. The disintegration of community and family life in refugee situations leads to the break-up of stable relationships and the disruption of social norms governing sexual behaviour. Women and children are frequently coerced into having sex to obtain basic needs, such as shelter, security, food and money. In a refugee situation, populations that have different rates of HIV/AIDS prior to becoming refugees may be mixed. Also many refugee situations are like

large urban settings and may create conditions that increase the risk of HIV transmission.[30]

The manual outlines steps to be taken at the outset of an emergency to limit the transmission of STDs: "Guarantee availability of free condoms; enforce universal precautions against HIV/AIDS transmission in health-care settings; and identify a person who will coordinate RH activities."[31] Once the situation stabilizes, comprehensive prevention, treatment, and care programs should be established based on systematic assessments of the infrastructure of the health services available to refugees, collection of baseline data on prevalence and patterns of transmission, and interviews with key informants on target groups for intervention, acceptability of preventive measures, and other information necessary to design effective programs.[32]

Experts emphasize that mandatory testing programs should not be implemented because they would violate the rights of refugees and displaced persons. Moreover, mandatory testing could put refugees in danger of *refoulement*. Voluntary counseling and testing (VCT) programs do have a role. The Refugee Reproductive Health Consortium advises that these basics must be in place, however: VCT programs should be available in the country of origin or asylum; informed consent must be obtained; pre- and post-test counseling must be available; confidentiality must be ensured; a method to confirm findings should be available; and there should be sufficient resources to train counselors and testers and carry out the programs.[33]

Particular attention needs to be given to the reproductive health needs of adolescents. A UNHCR/Women's Commission report describes the specific needs of younger refugees: early and unwanted pregnancy; complications of pregnancy and delivery; maternal mortality; STDs, including HIV/AIDS; unsafe abortions; rape, forced marriage, sexual enslavement, and other forms of sexual violence; and genital mutilation.[34] The field manual on reproductive health emphasizes that services for this population should be "user-friendly"; have competent staff who are friendly, welcoming, and nonjudgmental; promote trust and confidentiality; be free or low cost; be easily accessible; have flexible hours; be located in attractive facilities; and offer same-gender providers.[35]

Programs to address gender and sexual-based violence have grown along with other reproductive health services during the past decade. A global overview of gender-based violence (GBV) programs states:

> *Gender-based violence* is an umbrella term for any harm that is perpetrated against a person's will; that has a negative impact on the physical or psychological health, development, and identity of the person; and that is the result of gendered power inequities that exploit distinctions between males and females,

among males, and among females. Although not exclusive to women and girls, GBV principally affects them across all cultures. Violence may be physical, sexual, psychological, economic, or sociocultural.[36]

Gender-based violence programs generally advocate a multisectoral approach that takes into account prevention of abuses, the physical and psychological ramifications of violence, the potential need of the victim for a safe haven, the longer-term economic needs of vulnerable populations, the legal rights of victims, training of police and security personnel, and other similar issues. "No one sector, organization, or discipline has sole responsibility for preventing and responding to GBV. Everyone must work together to understand GBV and design strategies to address it. Most important, the term *everyone* includes the displaced communities; without active community involvement, GBV intervention cannot be fully successful."[37] Hence, the cooperation of all actors in refugee and displaced person settings is needed to address all of these elements of an effective response to GBV.

Too often, however, those responsible for overall security and protection see GBV as a "social" or "health" issue that they leave to those sectors to address. As a result, programs to deal with the aftermath of violence are more common than those that effectively prevent abuse. The assessment of GBV programs concludes:

> Protections for survivors of all forms of GBV are weak in every country profiled in this report. This is perhaps most true of unregistered refugees in Thailand and Pakistan, where the lack of host government recognition, the culture of violence against women that supports impunity for GBV-related crimes, and the extreme discrimination against women in general conspire to promote GBV crimes. Short-term funding and shifting donor priorities have also contributed to the inability of many programs to achieve the degree of expertise and conduct the level of comprehensive activities required to adequately combat GBV.[38]

Moreover, many GBV programs focus primarily on conflict-induced violence, particularly rape, and do not fully address other such forms of gender abuse as domestic violence and sexual exploitation.

Yet, more comprehensive programs do exist that can serve as a model for others. For example, Medica Zenica in Bosnia-Herzegovina began addressing war-related violence but quickly expanded its programming. It now has a counseling center, medical services, a hotline, and two safe houses with education, training, and microenterprise activities. Its research unit collects and analyzes data on gender-based violence to be used in prevention and advocacy programs.[39] Women in Burundian refugee camps in Tanzania undertook needs assessments that indicated that a breakdown in family, community, and government structures led to increased incidence of violence against women. Resulting programs include a drop-in center for violence survivors, at which their critical health and protection needs are addressed; community awareness building activities that reach out to men as well as women to discuss the prevalence and reasons for gender-based violence; social forums for women to discuss issues affecting their lives; and training for staff of service providers in the camps to alert them to issues surrounding gender based violence.[40]

Final types of programs that developed and grew in the 1990s involve the psychosocial needs of refugees and displaced persons. Women caught in conflict experience particular stresses that can affect their mental health as well as their ability to cope. As one study describes:

> While men are usually the active participants in war, women are often left to respond to the increasing chaos and the breakdowns in their families and communities. In war zones, women continue to be responsible for procuring and preparing food and for caring for children, the elderly, and the ill. They face survival issues every day with massive unemployment, dramatic price increases, lack of fuel, food shortages, shelling, and sniping. After women become refugees, they often live in poverty and feel powerless to reduce the stress in their families. Both women living in war and refugee women are often left to wonder if their husbands or children are alive or dead, leaving them in a living limbo (references deleted).[41]

Although centers have been established in many industrialized countries to address the post-traumatic stress and depression that these events may induce, Western psychiatric models are generally not followed in the developing countries in which most refugees and displaced persons are located. Rather, programs tend to focus on the fuller array of psychosocial needs that face the uprooted populations. They range from specialized mental health services to play, sports and other recreational groups for traumatized children to income generation activities for traumatized women. The aims are to prevent trauma and stressors that negatively effect mental health to the degree possible, and to strengthen the capacity of refugees to cope with the traumas and stressors when prevention fails.[42]

EDUCATION AND SKILLS TRAINING

Childhood Education

The right to education is universal. The Universal Declaration of Human Rights states explicitly, "Everyone has the right to education. Education should be free, at least in the elementary and fundamental stage." The UN Convention Relating to the Status of Refugees provides that: "Contracting States shall accord to refugees the same treatment as is accorded to nationals with respect to elementary education." The Executive Committee of the UNHCR has reaffirmed the fundamental right of refugee children to education and, in its thirty-eighth session called upon all states, individually and collectively, to intensify their efforts to ensure that refugee children benefit from primary education. Yet, the right to education continues to be abridged.

Millions of refugee and displaced children are without education, even at the elementary level. In 2000, fewer than 800,000 of an estimated 2.3 million children and adolescents receiving assistance from UNHCR were enrolled in schools. As a UNHCR report on education concluded: "One-third of refugee children (excluding infants) and adolescents in populations categorized as "UNHCR assisted" are in UNHCR-supported schooling, and that perhaps 40 percent are in school altogether."[43]

Educational coverage varies by refugee group, duration of displacement and other factors that influence the readiness of governments to support education, of parents to send children to school and of children to remain in school. Some experts believe that most refugee children receive some primary education, but the high dropout rates lower the overall coverage. Internally displaced children face even greater barriers to education, particularly when insecurity prevents them from attending school. As one report describes: "For over a decade and a half, war in northern Uganda and southern Sudan has caused the destruction of schools and the abduction and killing of students, teachers and school administrators. . . . Few young people see any clear paths to a steady job or income, and they feel their right to an education has become a luxury overshadowed by a constant preoccupation with meeting basic survival needs."[44] Fees charged for education in many developing countries may be prohibitive for displaced persons. During a site visit in Burundi, the author heard from displaced women that they could not afford fees, clothing, or books for their children. Some had requested financial assistance from the government and had been refused; most had not even asked.[45]

The situation for girls can be particularly problematic. A UNHCR evaluation found: "On a global basis, female refugee participation in education remains low, following patterns in countries of origin (ranging from 10 percent to 40 percent of students at the primary level, less in secondary and vocational studies, and only 25 percent of all students at the tertiary level)."[46] Poverty, which disproportionately affects women, further impedes their enrollment in schools. Families may fear that adolescent girls will be subject to greater sexual harassment if they leave compounds to go to school. Lack of appropriate clothing and sanitary materials may also impede educational attainment.

Afghan Girl, Kabul. (UNHCR/B. Press)

There have been successful programs to overcome the barriers to education for girls. In Pakistan, where Afghan girls traditionally had limited access to education, the 1990s saw major increases in girls' participation: "Coverage for girls has increased dramatically since the mid-1990s, thanks to a range of measures and perhaps general social change, possibly the desire of educated young refugee men for literate wives. It was much helped by the decision of the World Food Program to provide about 4 kg of edible oil per month to girls who attend school regularly. This helped to overcome the perception that it is pointless for Afghan girls to attend school, and too costly for poor families, in terms of requirements for decent clothing and so on."[47]

Even where refugee children have access to schools, the quality of education is often very poor. A 1986 report by the Economic Commission of Africa remains accurate:

> refugee teachers often lack adequate training, and the numbers of trained national personnel are inadequate for even national needs. Female teachers are often underrepresented in refugee schools, sometimes because few women had access to education in the country of origin. Materials are also in short supply, and a curious mixture of textbooks and teaching materials of different origins is found in refugee schools—whatever happens to be available rather than that which is suitable.[48]

When financial crises occur, education is often among the first activities to be cut.[49] A 2002 report on refugee schools in Tanzania found: "The program has suffered greatly from a lack of resources, and from an inability to access additional funds during the year to meet the needs of extra students. Communities are quick to make mud-brick walls for classrooms, but the UNHCR budget is insufficient to pay for corrugated sheet roofs, leading to oversized classes."[50]

Secondary and University Education

Opportunities for secondary and university education for refugees are limited in almost all locations. The Refugee Education Trust, established by the former UN High Commissioner for Refugees Sadako Ogata to promote secondary education, estimates that less than 3 percent of secondary school-aged refugees are enrolled. Factors listed by senior UNHCR staff included:

Legal barriers: National law in some countries may bar adolescents from accessing primary education.

Social pressures: For example, fourteen-year-olds may be laughed at when they attend school with eight-year-olds; it is very humiliating for a fourteen-year old to read more poorly than an eight-year-old.

Economic factors: Adolescent boys in particular are pressed to produce economically. Adolescent girls may be expected to perform the lion's share of domestic tasks, leaving little time to attend school or study out of school.

Cultural factors: War-affected communities themselves may not expect or value education for adolescent boys and girls. For many, education must be seen to lead to gainful employment or an improvement in livelihood. Boys' education is frequently valued over girls', and in some areas, there is a pressure for girls to marry quite young; and

Other obstacles: Lack of sanitary supplies and fear of embarrassment or humiliation may deter girls from attending school as does a lack of privacy should lavatories have to be shared with boys.[51]

UNHCR operates scholarship programs that allow a small number of refugees to obtain higher education. The Albert Einstein German Academic Refugee Initiative Fund, known as DAFI program, is a trust fund provided annually by the German government to UNHCR. "It aims to help needy and deserving refugee students who had attained excellent results in secondary school to continue their academic studies in developing countries." DAFI is the only scholarship available worldwide for refugee students at the tertiary level.

Skills and Literacy Training for Adult Women

Refugee situations often call for new skills and occupations for women. Many of the skills that women bring with them are not immediately or directly relevant to their experiences in refugee camps or settlements. Although many of their skills are transferable, refugee and displaced women often need training to undertake new roles in support of themselves and their families.

Education and skills training have numerous benefits for refugee and displaced women, as reported in the NGO Consultation on Refugee Women:

- increasing a woman's income-earning potential thus fostering self-sufficiency;
- furthering the ability of a woman to have some measure of control within the community in which she lives;
- providing skills which will be useful when—and if—the refugee returns home;
- enhancing the likelihood of resettlement;
- alleviating the oppressive monotony of camp life; and
- providing a measure of self-respect that may have been lost through years of unproductive exile.[52]

Refugee and displaced women face many of the same impediments to education and skills training as do children—inadequate resources, teachers, and classes. In addition, women face other barriers. Cultural constraints sometimes prevent women from accepting work or undertaking training that takes them out of the household. The culture may also set restrictions on the type of work that is considered to be appropriate for women. Practical problems also constrain enrollment, including need for day care and lack of time and energy after household work and/or jobs as a wage earner. Also, many skills training programs assume some level of prior education, most notably in terms of literacy. Refugee and displaced women may not qualify for such programs, having been discriminated against in their country of origin in obtaining elementary education.

Other constraints relate to the design and contents of training programs. In some cases, programs have been too far removed from the everyday life activities of the refugee women and have therefore appeared to be irrelevant to their needs. Some vocational training programs have focused on skills that are not marketable in the refugee context or follow traditional patterns that are not sustainable for income-production. A report on training programs for Burundi refugees in Tanzania followed traditional patterns: "Carpentry, building, and bicycle repair are for men; hair-*cutting* is done by men while hair-*dressing* is for women. Handicraft, home management, and baking are done in women's groups; and tailoring and typing have both male and female participants. An effort to widen the choice of access for women should be made."[53] Another evaluation of training programs recommended that: "Training programs therefore should be linked directly to concrete productive goals. For the majority of women refugees, it is more effective to combine training with the production of goods and/or services from the outset, rather than on training which is intended to lead to income earning at a later date, when training is completed."[54]

Despite these constraints, programs designed to redress illiteracy among refugees, including women and girls, have often met with great enthusiasm and success. For example, Women's Education for Advancement and Empowerment (WEAVE), based in Chiang Mai, works with Burmese refugees to train health care workers in MCH and HIV awareness. It provides nursery schools so that women are able to attend the classes.[55] The Lastavica Women's Safe House near Belgrade offers computer, English language, and catering courses. Training is also offered in hairdressing, sewing, and weaving.[56] After UNICEF staff distributing sanitary materials found that most of the Somali internally displaced women and girls were illiterate, the agency, working with an NGO women's network, launched a project to provide literacy and life-skills training.[57] A Palestinian women's center on the West Bank, supported by an Australian nongovernmental organization, launched a small business creation course. As a journalist described, "Fifteen or sixteen women, some of them nursing babies, circled around inevitable islands of butcher's paper. The excitement was both palpable and audible. It was a brainstorming session, designed to prompt the women to define their market environment and also to think about issues involved in setting up partnerships—the foundations for mutual trust for example. Over weeks, the course participants will design and construct a business."[58]

CONCLUSION

Improving protection and assistance programs for refugee and displaced women is an important first step in helping them resume their normal lives. As discussed in this chapter, some of the concrete steps that can be taken to increase access to assistance include:

- Refugee women should participate in all decisions about food distribution. To the extent possible, women should also be designated as the initial point of contact for emergency food distribution.
- The health status of women and children and the capacity to provide a nutritionally balanced diet should be monitored regularly to identify problems in the food ration or its distribution. Where nutritional deficiencies or declining nutritional status is detected, immediate steps should be taken to increase the calories or improve the nutritional contents of the rations.
- All health programs for refugees and displaced persons should emphasize the primary health care approach, which emphasizes preventive care. They should be assessed to ensure that they are culturally appropriate for refugee and displaced women, and that women have equal access to their services. Refugee and displaced women should participate fully in this process. Reproductive health services should be available in all refugee and displaced persons settings. Special attention should be paid to services needed by adolescent girls.
- Psychosocial services should be available to refugee and displaced women and children, particularly for victims of torture, rape, and other physical and sexual abuse.
- The right of all refugee and displaced children to primary education must be reaffirmed. Educational programs should be assessed and changes made, as needed, to ensure that girls have equal access to these programs.

- Educational and training programs for refugee and displaced women should be established. Refugee and displaced women should participate fully in the development and implementation of these programs.

As the next chapter will show, however, further efforts are needed if refugee and displaced women are to become financially independent of these assistance efforts.

NOTES

Full citations can be found in the select bibliography.

1. Paul Vallely, quoted in *Refugees* 23 (1985): 35.
2. Paul Spiegel, M. Sheik, P. Salama, and C. Crawford, "Health Programs and Policies Associated with Decreased Mortality in Displaced People in Post-Emergency Phase Camps: A Retrospective Study," *Lancet* (December 12, 2002).
3. UNHCR, *Handbook for Emergencies* (Geneva: UNHCR, 2000).
4. Sphere Project, *Humanitarian Charter and Minimum Standards in Disaster Response* (Geneva: Sphere Project, 1998).
5. UNHCR, *Handbook for Emergencies.*
6. Sr. Margaret Jane Kling, "A Case Study of Refugee Women and Health: San Jose, Calle Real, El Salvador," in *Working with Refugee Women: A Practical Guide,* 110.
7. UNHCR, *Guidelines on the Protection of Refugee Women* (Geneva: UNHCR, 1991). The guidelines were prepared by the author for UNHCR, based largely on the research undertaken for the first edition of *Refugee Women.*
8. Margaret Snyder, *Women: The Key to Ending Hunger* (New York: The Hunger Project, 1990), 4–5.
9. World Food Program, "Workshop: Women Beneficiaries Speak Out," Mapel, Bahr el Ghazal, Sudan, February 16–18, 2000.
10. U.S. Committee for Refugees, *Funding Crisis in Refugee Assistance: Impact on Refugees* (November 20, 2002).
11. Sphere Project, *Humanitarian Charter and Minimum Standards in Disaster Response.*
12. Women's Commission, *UNHCR Policy,* 27.
13. Women's Commission, *UNHCR Policy,* 28
14. Women's Commission, *UNHCR Policy.*
15. Women's Commission, *UNHCR Policy.*
16. Women's Commission, *UNHCR Policy.*
17. Sphere Project, *Humanitarian Charter and Minimum Standards in Disaster Response,* 252.
18. Sphere Project, *Humanitarian Charter and Minimum Standards in Disaster Response.*

19. Sphere Project, *Humanitarian Charter and Minimum Standards in Disaster Response*.

20. See, for example, the American College of Obstetricians and Gynecologists, "Female Circumcision/Female Genital Mutilation (FC/FGM) Fact Sheet." Available at www .acog.org/from_home/departments/dept_notice.cfm?recno=18&bulletin=1081 (n.d.).

21. Women's Commission, *UNHCR Policy*.

22. Lewin/ICF and Refugee Policy Group, *Promoting Mental Health Services for Refugees: A Handbook on Model Practices* (Washington, D.C.: Office of Refugee Resettlement, 1990), 12.

23. Annick Billard, "Women and Health in Afghan Refugee Camps," *Refugees* 2 (1983): 28.

24. Women's Commission, *UNHCR Policy*.

25. Mary B. Anderson and Peter J. Woodrow, *Rising from the Ashes: Development Strategies in Times of Disaster* (Boulder, Colo.: Westview Press, 1989), 24.

26. Women's Commission, *UNHCR Policy*, 30.

27. UNHCR, *Guidelines on the Protection of Refugee Women*.

28. Stability comes when crude mortality rate falls below 1 in 10,000 per day, when there are no major epidemics, and when the refugee population is not expected to repatriate or relocate within six months.

29. UNHCR, *Reproductive Health in Refugee Situations: An Inter-Agency Field Manual* (Geneva: UNHCR, 1999), 66.

30. UNHCR, *Reproductive Health in Refugee Situations*, 48.

31. UNHCR, *Reproductive Health in Refugee Situations*, 49.

32. UNHCR, WHO, and UNAID, *Guidelines for HIV Interventions in Emergency Settings* (Geneva: UNHCR, 1995).

33. Women's Commission for Refugee Women and Children, *Refugees and AIDS: What Should the Humanitarian Community Do?* (New York: Women's Commission for Refugee Women and Children, 2002).

34. UNHCR, *Work with Young Refugees to Ensure Their Reproductive Health and Well-Being: It's Their Right and Our Duty: A Field Resource for Programming with and for Refugee Adolescents and Youth* (Geneva: UNHCR, 2002).

35. UNHCR, *Reproductive Health in Refugee Situations*, 91.

36. Jeanne Ward, *If Not Now, When? Addressing Gender-Based Violence in Refugee, Internally Displaced, and Post-Conflict Settings: A Global Overview* (New York: Refugee Reproductive Health Consortium, 2002).

37. Beth Vann, "Gender-Based Violence: Emerging Issues in Programs Serving Displaced Populations," GBV Global Technical Support Project, JSI Research and Training Institute on behalf of the Reproductive Health for Refugees Consortium, September 2002.

38. Vann, "Gender-Based Violence," 13.

39. Vann, "Gender-Based Violence," 83.

40. Reproductive Health Outlook, "Refugee Reproductive Health, Program Examples." Available at www.rho.org/html/refugee_progexamples.htm#topofpage (n.d.).

41. James Jaranson, Susan Forbes Martin, and Solvig Ekblad, "Refugee Mental Health: Issues for the New Millennium," in *Mental Health United States: 2000*. Available at www.mentalhealth.org/publications/allpubs/SMA01-3537/chapter13.asp.

42. Alastair Ager, "Mental Health Issues in Refugee Populations: A Review," Working Paper of the Harvard Center for the Study of Culture and Medicine (July 1993).

43. UNHCR Evaluation and Policy Analysis Unit, Health and Community Development Section, *Learning for a Future: Refugee Education in Developing Countries* (Geneva: UNHCR, 2002), 6.

44. Women's Commission for Refugee Women and Children, *Against All Odds: Surviving the War on Adolescents: Promoting the Protection and Capacity of Ugandan and Sudanese Adolescents in Northern Uganda* (New York: Women's Commission for Refugee Women and Children, 2001), 24.

45. Women's Commission, *Out of Sight, Out of Mind*, 32.

46. Glen Dunkley, *Review of UNHCR's Refugee Education Activities* (Geneva: UNHCR, 1997).

47. Dunkley, *Review*, 54.

48. African Training and Research Centre for Women, 44.

49. UNHCR, "A Dark Cloud," *Refugees* 72 (1990).

50. UNHCR and Policy Analysis Unit, *Learning for a Future*, 51.

51. As reported in Women's Commission for Refugee Women and Children, *Untapped Potential: Adolescents Affected by Armed Conflict* (New York: Women's Commission for Refugee Women and Children, 2000).

52. Ninette Kelly, ed., *Working with Refugee Women*.

53. Erik Lyby, "Vocational Training for Refugees: A Case Study from Tanzania," in *Learning for a Future: Refugee Education in Developing Countries* (Geneva: UNHCR, 2002), 234.

54. Eve Hall, "Vocational Training for Women Refugees in Africa: Guidelines from Selected Field Projects: Training Policies Discussion Paper No. 26," (Geneva: International Labour Organization, 1988), 37.

55. Women's Commission for Refugee Women and Children, *Fear and Hope: Displaced Burmese Women in Burma and Thailand* (New York: Women's Commission for Refugee Women and Children, March 2000).

56. Women's Commission for Refugee Women and Children, *Refugee and Internally Displaced Women and Children in Serbia and Montenegro* (New York: Women's Commission for Refugee Women and Children, 2001).

57. Suba Mahalingam, "Education: Protecting the Rights of Displaced Children," *Forced Migration Review* 15 (October 2002).

58. Margaret Coffey, "Visiting Women on the West Bank." Available at www. austcare.org.au/content/west_bank_women.htm (n.d.).

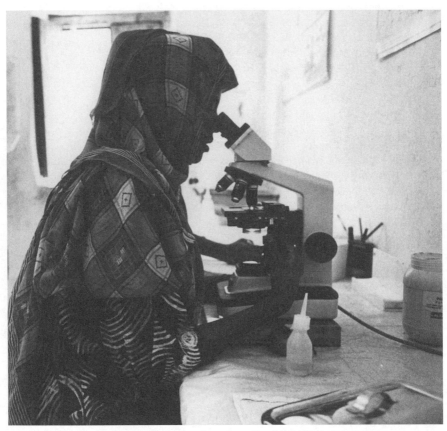

Somali Nurse in Bardera, Somalia. (UNHCR/B. Press)

5

Toward Greater Self-Sufficiency: Economic Activities and Income-Generating Projects

Parwin is the oldest widow in the widow's camp of Nasir Bagh in Pakistan, where she lives together with 300 families of refugee widows and their children. Her age has allowed Parwin to ask for work in the name of the other women, so that they can purchase those articles which are not included in the general aid distribution. A project set up by a voluntary agency supplies these refugee widows with the necessary material for quilt-making which it then purchases from them. Parwin and the other refugee widows feel that this is a first step towards self-sufficiency, and that they would be able, given the opportunity, to undertake many more income-generating activities.[1]

A basic need of many refugee and displaced women, particularly heads of households, is sufficient income to support their families. The extent to which refugee and displaced women are economic resources has often been underestimated. While household strategies for economic survival differ greatly, in all situations women play an important economic role.

Household strategies for economic survival vary depending on family composition, existing work opportunities, refugee and host country cultural constraints, and other factors. As Robert Chambers notes:

Very poor people often adopt one of two strategies for survival. Either they become totally reliant on one source; a patron, an employer or with refugees a government feeding program, or they cobble together a livelihood out of bits, improvising here, migrating there, fitting together a sequence of seasonal work to secure more or less adequate flows of food round the year.[2]

Especially in poorer families, the ability to engage in diverse economic activities can be crucial in enabling the family to survive. Refugee women in developing countries (like their host national counterparts) are an integral part of the family's economic activities whether those entail assisting in food production, marketing goods, or providing services such as cooking and laundry for other family members who engage in wage labor activities.

ECONOMIC ACTIVITIES

The main component of initial household survival strategies, especially for female-headed households, is the food ration. Most newly arrived refugees rely on rations as the key to survival during the first few weeks or months. If there are no opportunities to replace rations with other sources of income either in cash or in kind, refugees may remain dependent on rations for years.

Theoretically there are a number of ways that refugees can supplement their household income. They include: employment in the local economy or with assistance agencies; agricultural activities; bartering; establishment of trades or small businesses; and participation in skills training programs and formal income generation projects.

Refugees weigh several considerations when deciding what economic strategy to pursue. An important factor is the extent to which any activity will help obtain a *secure* source of income (either in cash or in kind) that enables them to survive. Lack of a safety net or financial cushion allows refugees only a small margin for financial risk taking. As shown in development studies, a small farmer will not use a new variety of plant until it is proven to be reliable. A parallel can be drawn to the refugees' reluctance to give up ration cards even if a job without rations might provide them with more income.

Refugees also take into account their hopes and prospects for repatriation and resettlement. Most refugees anticipate a return to their country of origin. Generally, they prefer not to commit significant resources to a project in the country of asylum, particularly if it calls for a long period of commitment, even if the investment could provide considerable return after a number of years. Typically income, if not used for survival, will be invested in portable products such as animals or gold.

If the principal goal of a refugee is resettlement in a third country, other strategies may be attractive. For example, a refugee seeking resettlement may prefer to work for a voluntary agency from the desired resettlement country. Or, a woman may accept a job as a domestic for an expatriate worker if she believes that this could lead to a recommendation for resettlement in a third country. Others hoping for resettlement may enroll in skills training or English language programs in the hopes of increasing their chances.

Prior education and skill levels of the refugees also affect the strategies they pursue. An individual who engaged in a trade or performed skilled labor may find it possible to work in the local economy, whereas a professional, such as a lawyer, may find few outlets in the country of first asylum. A refugee who speaks the language of expatriate agency staff will find it much easier to obtain employment with the agencies that operate in his or her area because of the ability to communicate.

Finally, culture constrains choices as to appropriate strategies, particularly with regard to women's economic choices. Women refugees whose culture generally prohibits employment outside the home will attempt to pursue strategies that permit them to work within their household compounds. Conflict can force households to make fundamental changes, however, in their economic coping strategies. One study of gender roles in conflict situations found that "Consistently across the case studies, women take on increased economic responsibilities within the household. The degree of change varies: in Mali sedentary communities, for example, reduced access to resources for both men and women mean neither can fulfill their gender roles adequately, while in Somalia, women often take over from men as principal breadwinners."[3]

The economic activities of refugee households fall into several categories:

Employment in the Local Economy or with Assistance Agencies

Refugees often seek jobs in the local economies of the host countries in which they find refuge. At times, they are given official permission to engage in such labor. In other situations, refugees work without formal authorization.

Women in developing countries must typically find employment in the informal sector of the economy. Refugee women in developing countries do the same. In general, refugee women who work in the local economy are within the service sector. For example, it is not uncommon to find a refugee woman supporting her family through her earnings as a domestic. These jobs are often a cornerstone in the household survival strategy for an extended family.

Assistance agencies are an important source of employment for refugees in developing countries. Typically these positions go to younger men who have the language skills to communicate with and relate to the expatriate staff in charge. These positions often offer a higher level of financial compensation than is usually available to refugees in the local market, relatively interesting nonmanual labor work (though the employees often feel they are overqualified for the position), more security, higher status, and other benefits such as an increased chance for resettlement to a third country.

The primary area of employment with assistance agencies for refugee women is in the health sector. In a number of cultures, it is more appropriate for women to seek medical advice from and be examined by other women. The employed women work in supplementary feeding programs, as traditional birth attendants, in mother/child health programs, as home visitors, particularly in public health education and outreach, as translators, etc. Following health programs, the second largest sector for employment is "women's projects," including income generation activities.

Agricultural Activities

Most refugees in developing countries are from rural areas. Prior to their flight the majority of these persons were involved in some kind of subsistence agricultural activities including crops and/or animals. It is not uncommon to hear refugees claim that the solution to their problems would be to receive either land to farm or animals to tend. If these resources were provided, they claim, there would not be the need for international assistance.

During the 1970s and 1980s, a strategy for attaining economic self-reliance, most commonly pursued in Africa and the People's Republic of China, was the creation of rural agricultural settlements for refugees. The primary goal was that refugees would become self-sufficient through agricultural activities. Refugee families received plots of land to farm. The families could then reconstruct to some degree a life similar to the one they left behind. These opportunities are far less prevalent today. Even countries such as Tanzania, which granted refugees relatively easy access to land in the 1970s, now limit refugee access to agricultural settlements. Whereas most of the Burundi refugees who came during the earlier decade were settled on agricultural land, those who arrived in the 1990s are required to live in UNHCR-assisted refugee camps.

Some agricultural opportunities exist in areas where large scale rural settlements are not possible or encouraged. Instead of creating rural settlements, the emphasis is on developing gardens next to the dwelling or compound. Refugee women are often involved in the tending of the garden plots. In these plots surrounding the house, refugees can raise vegetables to either supplement their diet or, if they choose, sell to earn some extra cash.

Market Activities

Many refugees who have no source of cash income have goods that the family can barter for other goods or sell in the camp or local markets. Small household items or jewelry that the refugees brought with them from home are common items that are valued in the markets. Refugees barter basic food rations if there are no other resources available to them.

These market activities can help refugees upgrade their standard of living or save them from having to purchase goods on the open market. They may also be a way to secure some small amount of cash income or other products for the household. Rarely would a refugee family be able to become self-reliant through this activity alone, but it can be the difference between bare survival and an acceptable standard of living.

Trades and Small Businesses

Skilled refugees often wish to use their skills in the host country. Other refugees wish to learn skills that will then help them generate income. Within refugee camps and settlements, as well as in neighboring villages and cities, there may be need for such skilled workers as bakers, mechanics, cobblers, tailors, and others.

While some refugees are successful in reestablishing themselves in business, other skilled workers need assistance. Since refugees may flee their countries on short notice and may have to travel very far on foot, skilled refugees are often unable to bring the tools of their trade with them. Without these items they must work as unskilled laborers or remain dependent on assistance. In Pakistan, during the 1980s, when the refugee population was at its peak, one agency estimated that over 10 percent of the approximately 2.8 to 3 million refugees were in this situation.[4]

INCOME-GENERATING PROJECTS FOR REFUGEE WOMEN

Special projects have been implemented as ways of addressing cultural constraints imposed on women who were seeking work outside the home. Such programs received strong support in the UNHCR *Guidelines on the Protection of Refugee Women* as a way to help refugee women avoid the sexual and other exploitation that comes from dependence on assistance programs. Income-generation programs are often seen as marginal activities, however. As a report on implementation of the UNHCR *Guidelines* reported: "As a consequence of lower donor funding, UNHCR has had to make painful choices. Funding for income generation has been reduced on the grounds that, while important to refugee well-being, this type of activity is not central to UNHCR's protection mandate. It is argued that other entities can manage the projects more efficiently. For example, in Africa in 2002, only $1.9 million in funding is available for income-generation activities among the 2.1 million refugees UNHCR assists. It is not clear how much of this funding reaches women."[5] The consequences of these funding cuts are by no means negligible, however: "The survival of camp-based Afghan women now depends essentially on the ability of male family members to find employment. In Pakistan, and likewise in Turkey, the lack of alternative sources of income has led some women to resort to prostitution in order to support their families."[6]

Activities of income-generating projects often focus on what are perceived as traditional women's activities. In Sudan, for example, income-generation projects for refugee women have included handicrafts, ceramics, and soap making. Handicraft projects have been a major income-generating activity for refugee women in Pakistan. Following an agreement signed in 1985 between UNHCR and the Pakistani government to promote self-help activities, a number of projects were implemented in refugee villages. Some met with the opposition of the male leadership but they were able to establish themselves by respecting *purdah*, the separation of male and female activities in public, and focusing on particularly vulnerable women, such as widows who had no other form of support.[7]

A number of problems have affected the success of income-generation programs. Too often, they have targeted marginal economic activities such as handicrafts. Women have generally not been involved in some of the larger projects that focus on reforestation, infrastructure development, or agricultural activities. Interestingly, in many of the cultures from which the refugee women come, women are traditionally involved in these activities, raising questions about whether Western biases about women's traditional role may be constraining choices. A 2001 consultation with refugee women led to the following observation by an Afghan refugee participant living in Pakistan: "Income generation projects and skills development must move beyond traditional areas of work for women. They should provide the appropriate skills to women or girls that are necessary for them to participate in and access new markets. Feasibility studies are particularly important to ensure that there will be markets for the goods produced and to ensure that income-generating projects are economically viable."[8]

Historically, few of the women's projects led to long-term economic self-sufficiency for the women involved although they do provide additional and often essential income. The programs suffer from such problems as: lack of clarity regarding the goals and objectives; lack of proper planning (skills assessment, market research, identification of appropriate participants, etc.); excessive administrative costs and/or inadequate funding; unrealistic timelines; and inadequate consultation with the refugee community.[9]

These programs do demonstrate, however, that refugee women are interested in increasing their incomes and will participate in economic activities outside the home if given the chance. And, some programs have provided substantial support for the economic endeavors of refugee women. For example, an early income-generation project, the Port Sudan small-scale enterprise development program, provided loans, business training, and advice. Its implementer, ACORD, has a policy of reaching out to assist women refugees. About 40 percent of their loans went to women-run enterprises.

The program provided tools and/or equipment on a hire purchase basis; loans for working capital, ranging from $60 to $200 at a time, with a maximum repayment period of two months; and short-term loans, preferably to groups, for a maximum of $15, which must be repaid in one month. These loans are primarily to buy basic raw material in bulk. In addition, the program provided workshops and market facilities for a small monthly rental. In the case of communal shelters for women vendors, rental was paid on a daily basis. A management consultancy service, for a small fee based on the net income of the business, gave basic training in business management and monitored the progress of the enterprise for the period of the loan repayment.

The factors influencing the effectiveness of efforts to increase the economic self-reliance of refugee women fall into several major categories: the commitment of the assistance community to income-generation activities; economic and legal constraints; and planning and implementation issues.

Commitment to Income Generation

A major factor in the success of efforts to increase income for refugee women is the receptivity and seriousness with which donors, governments, and project implementers support the income-generating projects. While a great deal of lip service is paid to the concept of self-help, there is little evidence of serious commitment to ensuring the long-term effectiveness of income-generating projects.

Projects for women have fallen victim to the same pressures that apply generally with regard to development approaches for refugees. Efforts to increase self-reliance of refugees in general are, in many ways, a stepchild of international endeavors in the Third World. UNHCR focuses its primary attention on assistance and protection for refugees, expending relatively small amounts on projects to enhance self-support. As new crises arise and funding for refugee assistance declines, donors often target their support for emergency relief. The traditional development organizations that have greater expertise in this area—UN Development Program, for example—do not have the mandates to provide ongoing support for refugee-related projects. Host governments are, at best, ambivalent about these projects, fearing that the refugees may remain permanently within their borders.

Most often the involvement of women in income-generating activities has been through projects clearly defined as "women's" programs. There are many reasons to classify projects by gender. Most specifically, women-only projects provide a greater opportunity to address the cultural constraints on women's participation in income-generating activities. Some of the most successful projects, in terms of recruitment of participants, spent considerable time determining culturally appropriate ways to conduct classes or provide workspace to women.

While women-specific projects provide some advantages, as implemented they have tended to present problems as well. In most locations, the trend is to involve women in marginal economic activities because they are seen as traditional or acceptable ones. The universal emphasis on handicrafts and sewing projects is illustrative.

The agencies implementing projects vary greatly in their approach to income generation. Some agencies build on previous experience with women and development programs, and they are therefore fully committed to economic as well as social ends. Others approach the issue from a social service perspective which, when combined with little experience or expertise in designing projects with economic objectives, can lead to minimal achievement of economic ends.

A holistic approach that recognizes the special circumstances of refugee and displaced women, and is realistic in establishing economic goals, works best. In assessing one such program, the evaluator concluded: "The income generation/micro-credit projects have had a positive impact on the lives of refugee women. From the beginning, hiring practices sought a gender balance so that half the business extension agents were women. The program provides business training and small loans to groups, preferably groups of women, who qualify for a larger loan once they repay the initial loan. The projects incorporate some special attributes such as training on conflict resolution, trauma counseling, a peace-building component as well as carefully-crafted outreach to survivors of sexual violence."[10]

Economic and Legal Constraints

Even where the commitment to increased self-reliance of refugee women is unimpeachable, projects face difficult economic constraints. Many projects have been implemented in countries facing their own economic crises. High levels of inflation soon rendered planning budgets obsolete. Transportation costs have been high, if transportation is even available. Refugee camps and settlements and the surrounding villages are often poor, providing inadequate markets for products produced by project participants. Local unemployment has made it difficult for refugees to compete with local inhabitants for scarce jobs, even if they receive appropriate training.

Even relatively successful programs run into problems resulting from economic inadequacies. In western Sahara, the camp government promoted textile production capability to increase refugee self-reliance. However, the economic activities were beset by: "Frequent and extended disruption of production, lack of short term incentives and lack of institutional encouragement for experimentation in design."[11]

Beyond these economic constraints are legal ones. Refugees often do not qualify for work permits or business licenses. Where these are available to refugees, the procedures for obtaining one may be long, difficult, and costly. Some of the implementing agencies do not have the resources or will to go through these processes on behalf of participants. In addition, refugees are generally not allowed to own land or standing structures; they need to rent them, often at exorbitant costs, from local residents. Travel documents are a third limitation. Refugees may not receive permission to travel to markets. The legal constraints make it difficult, if not impossible, for refugee businesses to survive. In some cases, the continued dependence on international assistance is caused by legal pressures as much as economic ones. As a "project," the income-generation activity could be implemented, but as an independent business it would be illegal or on shaky legal basis.

While these economic and legal limitations are very serious ones, some projects have been more successful than others at addressing them. A 1987 study by the author and her colleagues found that the use of cooperatives was an important factor in helping projects succeed in both the Sudan and Costa Rica, for example.

The Sudanese government allowed refugee endeavors to register as official cooperatives. This gave the refugees access to goods, such as sugar, at the official price. Cooperatives could also provide a needed economic base for the funding of business activities. The Wad Awad cooperative is a good example. Established in 1981, the cooperative negotiated with the Sudanese Cooperative Office and the Commission on Refugees for permission to open a shop. It also obtained control over a grinding mill, received a lorry from UNHCR, and opened a welding shop. Plans were underway at the time of the study to provide electricity and ambulance/transport service. All of these activities were organized by the refugees, and they were legal and recognized as such by the government.

In Costa Rica, the limitations on the number of aliens employed by a business did not apply to cooperatives. Therefore, projects utilizing cooperative structures were not subject to these same problems in hiring refugee workers as would be other businesses in the country. Some of the self-sufficiency activities examined by the study—for example, a fisheries project that will provide jobs for both men and women—envisioned use of cooperatives composed equally of Costa Ricans and Nicaraguans. The project planners expected to receive permission for their activities because of the legal structure chosen, as well as the involvement of host country nationals.

Other projects have bypassed legal constraints on their implementation through direct negotiations with officials of the host government. Here, an important ingredient is trust. In one case, for example, an indigenous voluntary agency was able to implement training programs in camps where the official policy strongly prohibited these activities and foreign agencies were denied permission to begin similar activities. In other cases, a particularly savvy administrator understood the loopholes available in local laws and took advantage of them for the benefit of the project.

Planning and Implementation

Certain approaches of planning and implementation appear to have contributed to the success of income-generation projects.

Clearly Defined Objectives

The concept of an income-generation activity can have different connotations to different individuals. While variation, in and of itself, is not a problem, it can lead to confusion about the basic nature and objectives of the project. Many income-generation projects contained other worthy objectives such as literacy or health and nutrition training. Those projects which keep income generation as the primary goal, regardless of what the secondary objectives are, seem to accomplish the most for participants, at least as far as income is concerned. In part, income generation for refugee women has established a bad track record because nonincome-generation projects (i.e., social service projects) have been labeled under the rubric income generation even though their economic objectives were secondary.

It appears that at a minimum an income-generation project should be committed to the following objectives: First, the *primary* goal is to generate income for the participants. Second, the income generated should be in proportion to the amount of time and energy which the refugee women must invest in the activity. Otherwise time is lost for which they could have engaged in other potentially more productive activities. Third, staff and participants must have a mutual understanding of the project's goals and outcomes. The most important factor is that refugee women and project staff have a clear understanding of why the project is being implemented. Other goals can be included in the project, but, as discussed below, mechanisms such as progress evaluations are needed to keep multigoal projects on track.

Knowledge of the Population

Agencies implementing income-generation projects must conduct systematic needs assessments and obtain demographic breakdowns of the population they hope to serve. Relying on staff perception of need and the resources that refugees would bring to the programs is insufficient. Agencies that possess a good knowledge of the refugee population are better able to target the resources to the most needy and deserving. They are also able to build on the existing skills and interests of the refugees. Otherwise, problems develop. In several cases examined by the author, for example, agencies had assumed that the refugee women would be interested in sewing workshops. They then had difficulty recruiting participants because the refugee women, in fact, had little prior experience. Even where the projects did recruit participants, we heard from the refugees that they would not have independently chosen this activity had others been available.

Projects must also be clear about the people they were targeting to participate. A range of options is available. Projects can aim at increasing self-sufficiency for the individual, the family, the project, or the settlement. Also, an agency can target the project for women only, the whole family or an integrated group. Agencies need to examine the appropriateness of their employment strategy vis-à-vis their target group, however. For example, if projects target single heads of households and require full-time participation, they should not offer part-time wages that are insufficient to support a whole household. While part-time employment may work if aimed at the second wage earner within a family, it causes hardships for participants who then have no time to earn supplemental income.

Addressing Cultural Constraints

It is essential for programs to differentiate between real versus imagined cultural constraints. Agencies with a better understanding of and rapport with the community are able to more effectively implement income-generation programs for women. They can avoid obvious problems or let the women decide whether the proposed activity would cause difficulties for them. For example, when working with Afghans in Pakistan, it was essential that men and women have separate work facilities. This requirement did not mean, however, that men and women could not work on the same project. Some agencies implemented projects involving both sexes but devised ways to keep men and women workers apart where cultural dictates demanded it.

Similarly, a home gardening project in Sudan showed the need to probe for information about the true meaning of presumed cultural constraints. Men said that the women would not be interested in the home gardening project. The women, however, indicated interest and said it would not be a problem since the gardens were next to their houses. Efforts should be made by the agencies to preserve the refugees' traditions, but they simultaneously have to guard against overinterpreting what the tradition may require.

Another important factor is the ability of both expatriate and local staff to communicate with the refugee women. Appropriate language skills have been stressed by development groups as an important factor not only in designing projects but also in overcoming problems and in managing disputes. This has often translated into hiring local staff. When working with refugee women, however, expatriate staff must keep in mind that even if the local staff speaks the official language of the country, they still may not be able to communicate with large numbers of refugee women. It may be that only refugee staff will have the necessary communication skills.

Project Implementation

Many income-generation projects for women suffer from implementation problems. Evaluations have shown that feasibility studies were too rarely undertaken before the design of a project was finalized in order to determine early on which problems would be faced. In some cases, the problems could have been anticipated and solved; in others, the project should have been scrapped.

Several problems seem to be common occurrences. Among the most commonly related obstacles to effective program implementation have been: marketing difficulties; difficulties in obtaining raw materials; quality control problems; transportation problems in getting goods to markets, or alternatively, getting workers to jobs; inadequately trained staff; lack of skills among participants; lack of monitoring and evaluation; and inappropriate funding cycles which provided too little time for projects to become operational and effective before further funding decisions were to be made.

CONCLUSION

Despite various obstacles to the involvement of refugee women in income-generating programs, their interest and willingness to participate in such economic activities is clear. From both necessity and desire to better their lives, refugee women undertake to engage in outside employment, agricultural efforts, and other income-producing activities. Imaginative programs are needed to help ensure their access to an important means of economic support. Steps that can be taken to ensure access to such programs include:

- ensuring the full participation of refugee and displaced women in the design and implementation of income-generation programs;
- giving high priority to integrating refugee and displaced women into all development plans. Projects that target women should be implemented where there are cultural or other barriers to overcome that do not equally affect men;
- monitoring projects carefully to make sure they provide sufficient household income and do not focus on marginal economic activities; and
- providing technical assistance to agencies implementing economic projects to ensure effective planning, implementation, monitoring, and evaluation.

NOTES

Full citations can be found in the select bibliography.

1. UNHCR, *UNHCR and Refugee Women: Employment* (Geneva: UNHCR, n.d.).
2. Robert Chambers, *Rural Refugees in Africa: Past Experience, Future Pointers* (New York: Ford Foundation, 1984).
3. Judy El-Bushra, Asha El-Karib, and Angela Hadjipateras, "Gender-Sensitive Programme Design and Planning in Conflict-Affected Situations," ACORD, ESCOR Project R 7501. Available at www.acord.org.uk/Publications/G&CResearch/ (January 2002).
4. Susan Forbes Martin and Emily Copeland, *Making Ends Meet? Refugee Women and Income Generation* (Washington, D.C.: Refugee Policy Group, 1987).
5. Women's Commission, *UNHCR Policy*, 30–31.
6. Women's Commission, *UNHCR Policy*.
7. During 1990, there were a number of attacks on Afghan women's projects in Pakistan, putting into question the viability of these approaches as well as raising serious questions about the protection of women refugees.
8. UNHCR and Women's Commission for Refugee Women and Children, *Respect Our Rights: Partnership for Equality, Report on the Dialogue with Refugee Women*.
9. See for example, Martin and Copeland, *Making Ends Meet?* as well as Eve Hall, "The Integrated Refugee Camp Development Project in Somalia," in *Working with Refugee Women: A Practical Guide*, ed. N. Kelly.
10. Susan J. Purdin, "Lessons from West Africa," *Sexual Health Exchange,* no. 2. Available at www.kit.nl/information_services/exchange_content/html/2000_2_lessons_from_west_afric.asp (2000).
11. Angharad Thomas and Gordon Wilson, "Technological Capabilities in Textile Production in Sahrawai Refugee Camps," *Journal of Refugee Studies* 9, no. 2 (June 1986): 182–98.

Two Sisters from Myanmar Reunited after Exile in Bangladesh. (UNHCR/A. Hollmann)

6

Durable Solutions: Repatriation and Integration

A tall thin man emerges cautiously from the shadows. He walks into the glare of the headlights, and looks unbelievingly at the young woman in front of him. It is Lydia, the youngest of his nine children. "I had heard that people were coming back," the old man tells us. "And when I heard the car approaching, I thought to myself, maybe it's her. Perhaps she really has come home. But I still can't believe it." As he speaks, other members of the family—brothers, sisters, uncles, and aunts—appear from the darkness, whooping with surprise and delight as they catch sight of their long-lost relative.[1]

A major goal of the refugee system is to find durable solutions for those who have been forced to flee their homes. There are three such solutions—voluntary return to one's country of origin, settlement in a country of first asylum, and resettlement in a third country. The most desired is voluntary return to one's country of origin, hopefully after conditions have changed sufficiently to permit safe and dignified reintegration (see tables 6.1 and 6.2). Refugees able to go back to their homelands already know the culture and lifestyles there, which means they can avoid the painful transitions that other refugees must face. Moreover, they often have family or community resources in place to aid them socially and economically upon their return. Particularly when displacement was caused by ethnic cleansing, return reestablishes the right of people to settle and live safely in their home communities.

Where voluntary return is unlikely, at least for an extended period of time, the next best option for most refugees is settlement in neighboring countries. Neighboring countries often share cultural values and refugees may be able to live with ethnic cousins. Physical and economic conditions are also likely to be similar, thus requiring less need for major adjustment to new circumstances.

Table 6.1. Voluntary Repatriation of Refugees by Region of Origin, 1992–2001 (Thousands)

Region	1992	1993	1994	1995	1996	1997	1998	1999	2000	2001	Total
Africa	510.6	773.5	2,531.9	665.1	1,648.9	628.2	695.3	291.9	253.6	266.8	8,266.0
Asia	1,668.2	77.0	493.6	496.5	299.9	155.6	162.7	455.3	350.5	49.2	4,208.6
Europe	43.5	0.0	0.2	0.8	104.7	138.9	154.1	849.5	162.6	146.2	1,600.6
Latin America and the Caribbean	18.5	9.9	10.1	11.1	7.3	3.7	4.2	2.2	0.7	0.2	57.8
North America	—	0.0	—	—	—	—	—	—	0.0	—	0.0
Oceania	—	—	—	—	—	—	—	—	—	—	—
Various/unknown	2.4	0.7	1.2	0.2	15.8	—	0.1	0.2	0.0	0.0	20.6
Total	**2,243.1**	**861.1**	**3,037.0**	**1,173.7**	**2,076.6**	**926.6**	**1,016.4**	**1,599.1**	**767.5**	**462.4**	**14,163.6**

Figures are based on departure and arrival records.
Source: UNHCR *Statistical Yearbook,* 2001.

Table 6.2.   Significant Voluntary Repatriations 2002

To	From	Number
Afghanistan	Iran and Pakistan	1,800,000
Angola	Congo-Kinshasa, Zambia, and others	80,000
Burma	Bangladesh and Thailand	1,760
Burundi	Tanzania	50,000
Central African Republic	Congo-Kinshasa	15,000
Croatia	Yugoslavia and Bosnia	11,000
East Timor	Indonesia	32,000
Eritrea	Sudan	20,000
Iraq	Iran	1,145
Kazakhstan	Uzbekistan and others	35,000
Liberia	Côte d'Ivoire and Sierra Leone	20,000
Namibia	Botswana	1,000
Nigeria	Cameroon	8,000
Rwanda	Congo-Kinshasa, Tanzania, and Burundi	30,000
Senegal	Gambia and Guinea-Bissau	5,000
Sierra Leone	Guinea, Liberia, and others	90,000
Somalia	Ethiopia, Kenya, and Djibouti	20,000
Sri Lanka	India	1,000
Sudan	Uganda	2,000
Tajikistan	Kazakhstan, Kyrgyzstan, and others	1,100
Yugoslavia	Germany and Switzerland	3,100

Source: World Refugee Survey 2003, U.S. Committee for Refugees.

Repatriation and permanent settlement in a neighboring country may not be possible for some refugees. In these cases, resettlement to a third country may be the best solution both for the protection of the refugees and as the only possible durable solution to their situation. Resettlement brings with it different issues and problems for refugee women than do the other two solutions; it is discussed in a separate chapter.

PEACE, RECONSTRUCTION, AND REPATRIATION

Voluntary repatriation in safety and dignity stands out as the preferred solution to any refugee situation. Since World War II, and particularly since the end of the Cold War, that solution has found reality in a number of situations in which massive numbers of refugees have been able to return to their home countries. Following the declaration of independence in many former colonies or territories of other countries, returns have been common. The most massive repatriation program involved refugees returning to Bangladesh after its formation in December 1971. Within four months more than 10 million refugees returned to their homes. Countries seeing significant returns just during the past fifteen years include Afghanistan, Cambodia, Mozambique, Ethiopia, Nicaragua, El Salvador, Guatemala, Bosnia, and Kosovo. In a number of these situations, however, the peace that brought return was short lived and further displacements occurred in subsequent years.

It is generally assumed that refugee women will be a force for voluntary return if given the opportunity. Anecdotal information lends support to this idea. Cambodian, Afghan, and Mozambique women spoke eloquently of their desire to return even before the conflicts in their countries abated enough to permit repatriation to take place. Refugee women still in neighboring countries, as well as those who are internally displaced, continue to dream of return to their home communities. They hope to see their parents before it is too late. They also tell of their aspirations for their children, which revolve around return and reconstruction of their home countries. They speak as well of their concern that their children and their children's children will never see the home country again.[2] Refugee women also express their fears about return. As one report notes, "They are longing for their home country but their first condition for going back is that there must be peace."[3]

When the Cold War ended, refugee experts spoke of a year, then a decade, of repatriation. While the wars, repression, and poor economic conditions that displaced millions of people persisted, repatriation did become a reality for many who came from newly democratizing states, particularly in the former Communist bloc. As foreign troops withdrew from a number of conflict areas—for example, Afghanistan and Cambodia—returns became reality for millions more refugees. Resolutions to long-standing civil wars, no longer supported by the Cold War superpowers, allowed still more return to take place throughout the world.

Even with the promising developments of the 1990s, repatriation and reintegration proved to be a difficult, sometimes elusive, solution for many refugees. In several countries, conflicts involving outside military forces gave way to internal conflicts that have been no less bloody than the ones that forced the refugees into exile. That has certainly been the situation in Afghanistan and Cambodia. Refugee returnees often found it impossible to return to their home communities, where landmines, ethnic rivalries, continued conflict, and other problems impeded their safety. For many refugees, returns were precipitated by deterioration of conditions in countries of asylum, rather than improvements in their home countries. Certainly, returns from then Zaire to Rwanda, Somalia to Ethiopia, and Côte d'Ivoire to Liberia have been in this category. Internally displaced persons (IDPs) have also returned to their home villages because conflict has spread to their places of refuge, even though they may be subsequently redisplaced as the patterns of conflict shift once more.

Even when peace comes, the problems of reconstruction are formidable. The conflicts that have caused uprooting in many developing countries have also caused the destruction of the economy and much of the infrastructure of the countries. The home countries, for their part, may be ambivalent about the return of their citizens. On the one hand, the willingness of people to repatriate is a potent symbol of the legitimacy of a new government, particularly one that is striving to show that it has established democratic institutions. On the other hand, many countries coming out of conflict do not have adequate economic resources to reintegrate their citizens—that is, provide jobs, housing, medical care, food, etc. Also, citizens who have stayed through the fall of one regime and the emergence of a new one may be antagonistic toward the expenditure of scarce resources in assisting those who fled. Peace agreements may have paid lip service to the return of minorities to land now held by other groups, as was the case in the Dayton agreement that ended conflict in Bosnia, but delicate power-sharing arrangements may work against such returns. Conversely, it may be recognized to be in the interest of those who remain behind for the exiles to stay abroad. Remittances from migrants who have gone to industrial countries, for example, provide an important source of economic support regardless of the reasons for migration.

Return from industrialized countries is particularly problematic. Repatriation is clearly the goal of many refugees and displaced persons who have settled in industrialized countries as it is for those who have been in developing ones. It is not unusual for such migrants to proclaim their intentions to return to their homelands as soon as the violence abates and/or repressive governments are replaced. Yet, the road from hope to actual return is often difficult for those who have been settled in Europe and North America. Giving up economic and physical safety in their new home countries for the unsettled conditions in their former places of residence may prove too daunting, particularly for families whose children have integrated successfully into their new environment.

If and when voluntary return takes place, the assistance needs of the returnees will be great. Beatrice Manz has written about repatriation of Guatemalan refugees: "For any repatriation to be successful, the refugees need to regain their economic means of survival, which means regaining their land and reintegration into the local economies. They will need economic aid to farm that land and assistance must be guaranteed until the refugees have achieved self-sufficiency."[4]

Development assistance will undoubtedly play an important role in facilitating reintegration of refugees and displaced persons. After what may be decades of civil strife and economic dislocation, many countries do not have the resources or capacity to easily accommodate returnees. A number of factors will influence planning for potential repatriation, including development programs aimed at assisting refugees to reintegrate.

The scope and scale of repatriation/return efforts—It is important to comprehend the full scope of likely repatriation/return programs. These programs differ in size of the refugee and displaced population; the period of time during which return takes place; the number of places from and to which the refugees move; the number of organizations providing assistance; the amount of funding available for assistance programs; and so forth.

Contexts in which return takes place—Return programs differ in the conditions to which the refugees and displaced persons will return. In some situations, relative peace may have been secured prior to any return, whereas in other situations continued fighting and targeted repression is likely to take place. Understanding the relationship between the uprooted populations and military forces on both sides to a conflict is also necessary to understanding the outcome of return programs in some locations.

Assistance to returnees—Thorough needs assessments must be conducted to determine what types of assistance will be needed by returnees; what agencies should be involved in providing assistance (intergovernmental organizations, the country of return, nongovernmental agencies, other governments through bilateral contributions, etc.); what, if any, coordination will be needed; and which agency should provide it.

Relationship between humanitarian assistance and reconstruction efforts—Return programs cannot be implemented in a vacuum because they are an essential part of the process of reconstructing the home country. It is necessary to make decisions early on as to how best to coordinate assistance to refugees and displaced persons and efforts to reconstruct the country.

Protection of returnees—While some returns take place without a guarantee of safety, it is preferable to know ahead of time what provisions are in place for ensuring the protection of returnees prior to their repatriation. Provisions are also needed to ensure the voluntary nature of return. And, likely physical protection problems, such as land mines, must be identified and steps taken to address them.

Full set of population movements—Return of refugees may be only one part of an exchange of population following significant changes in the political life of a country. It is necessary to understand the movement patterns of those who had been internally displaced within the borders of the country; out-migration of those who are on the losing side of any settlement; migration of people jeopardized by continued fighting; and migration to other countries of people unable to economically support themselves in the home country.

The needs and potentialities of subpopulations of returnees—As in other aspects of refugee programming, return has differential impacts depending on the gender and age of returnees. Specific issues pertaining to women and children must be identified and plans made to address their needs and help them participate fully in the repatriation process.

As with other programs affecting refugee and displaced women, participation in the planning process is essential to ensuring that the specific impacts on women and children are identified. The UNHCR *Handbook on Voluntary Repatriation: International Protection* promotes such involvement, particularly during the planning period:

> Women should be given adequate opportunity to express their views on the repatriation as part of any designated representatives of the refugee community, as individuals, and as a group. Refugee women should be actively involved in the planning and implementation of the information campaign (e.g., through participation in information committees). In contexts where women are unlikely to participate in meetings also attended by men, separate information meetings and counseling sessions should be set up for refugee women. If information committees are established, a women's information committee is needed as well. It is important to note that the principal concerns expressed by women in connection with repatriation may not be identical to those voiced by men. If this has been identified, the information needs of women have to be addressed with the same attention as the concerns and questions raised by men.[5]

Involving women adequately and effectively in repatriation decisions is a serious goal, but it is one that too often is ineffectively carried out. A June 2002 report to the General Assembly on the global consultations on international protection organized by UNHCR concluded: "Regarding planning for repatriation, many delegations stressed the need to give refugees, especially refugee women, an active voice in planning for both repatriation and reintegration-related activities. It was also recommended that such planning take due account of the needs of the most vulnerable, including unaccompanied and separated children, the disabled, the elderly, as well as single-headed households."[6]

Repatriation and the Protection of Women

The UNHCR emphasizes that voluntary return must be in safety and dignity. The *Handbook on Voluntary Repatriation: International Protection* notes that "among the elements of 'safety and dignity' to be considered are: the refugees' physical safety at all stages during and after their return including en route, at reception points and at the destination; the need for family unity; attention to the needs of vulnerable groups; the waiver or, if not possible, reduction to a minimum of border crossing formalities; permission for refugees to bring their movable possessions when returning; respect for school and planting seasons in the timing of such movements; and freedom of movement." Recognizing that the protection of refugee women and children may require special arrangements, the *Handbook* includes a special box reminding repatriation planners: "Make appropriate arrangements for the physical safety of unaccompanied women and women heads of household in departure, transit or reception centers (such as separate areas close to the relevant infrastructure with adequate security arrangements, lighting)."[7]

Many of the physical protection issues facing refugee and displaced women and children on flight hold similar potential on return, particularly where return is spontaneous and unassisted. Women and children may be subject to the same type of physical and sexual abuse from border guards, for example, in crossing the border back to their home country. Internally displaced persons may face similar problems in returning to their home villages. Other protection problems arise when refugee and displaced women remain in camps while their husbands and sons scout out the prospects for return: "In many cases, Afghan families send the men or older boys ahead to check land and property, and to investigate whether it is safe for the entire family to return. When this happens, Afghan women are left on their own in refugee camps and villages, and may be at greater risk."[8]

Once back, the returnees may experience harassment or more serious protection problems from the authorities and/or villagers who remained at home. Issues of landownership, for example, may generate tensions resulting in violence. Where male members of a family have been killed, women returnees may face special problems in reclaiming their property.

While some return occurs after a peace settlement has been implemented, others take place during periods of continuing hostilities. Moreover, the government that initiated actions against the refugees and displaced persons, and thereby led to their flight, may still be in charge of the country. The presence of a large number of unexploded mines in conflict zones has been shown to be a major protection problem.

Responsibility for protection of returnees is often unclear. Since individuals are once more within their own country, their government should have the principal protection function. Yet, return often occurs under circumstances in which the goodwill of the government cannot be assumed. The role of international organizations is likely to be limited, however, and subject to the willingness of the government to permit their presence. Nongovernmental organizations also require permission of the countries of origin, but their presence may be desired if the NGOs are able to bring resources with them. Often, NGOs by their very presence play an important protection role because they are the only foreign presence able to monitor possible abuses.

A further protection problem involves the actual decision to return. Often, camp leaders make decisions on return and there may be little opportunity for women to express their views either as a group or as individuals. This can cut two ways. In some situations, women who would like to return to their homes are unable to because male leaders have determined that no one should repatriate. For example, along the Thai-Cambodian border during the 1980s, in eastern Zaire in the mid-1990s and West Timor in the late 1990s, many women and children were in effect captives of the resistance groups that controlled the camps.

Under other circumstances, women may be compelled to return "voluntarily" because of reductions in assistance, poor living conditions, and physical abuse. A delegation examining the situation of Vietnamese women and children in Hong Kong reported in 1990:

> It appears from our discussions with women who have chosen to return that some Vietnamese are being coerced into doing so under the guise of "voluntary repatriation." Most of those agreeing to voluntary return have done so before undergoing screening [to determine if they meet refugee criteria], often citing the horrendous conditions in Hong Kong as their reason for volunteering to return.[9]

To complicate matters, women are not always given information needed to make an informed choice. The same delegation to Hong Kong commented: "In general, there is insufficient counseling for those asked to make as serious a decision as voluntary repatriation. . . . The Vietnamese have many questions about the fate that awaits them but little information about the experiences of those who preceded them."[10]

To address these deficiencies, the UNHCR *Handbook on Voluntary Repatriation* emphasizes the importance of providing adequate information to women, as described above, as well as seeking input from women to determine if they agree to decisions on return. The *Handbook* states that family interviews are generally the preferred way to determine the voluntariness of decisions, but it alerts interviewers that there may be circumstances in which women should be separately questioned. In particular, separate interviews may be justified when the female spouse has been politically active, is of a different ethnic or religious group than her husband, or has had personal experiences, such as sexual violence, that would prevent her from returning in safety and dignity.[11]

The UNHCR *Guidelines* on the prevention of sexual violence against refugee women outline further steps that can be taken to enhance the physical security of returnees:

- Promote and implement family reunification in the pre-repatriation stage.

- Ensure that families, including extended families, can travel as a unit. The same applies for groups of refugees, who have developed a social network in the camp (e.g., groups of female-headed households and un-accompanied women) who wish to return to the same destination. This could be ensured by linking together voluntary repatriation forms for joint travel.
- Ensure that refugee women, on an equal basis with refugee men, are provided with a viable opportunity to declare individually their desire to return or opt out of a voluntary repatriation, and have equal access to information on which to base their decision.
- Ensure the physical safety of areas, such as reception centers and transit camps and their facilities.
- Ensure that protection activities focused on returnees give high priority to assessing the safety of returnee women. Special attention should be paid to especially vulnerable individuals, for example the disabled, pregnant women, and unaccompanied minors, by identifying them early in repatriation planning and developing specific procedures to transport and receive them.
- Ensure that protection and field officers monitoring the return have a thorough knowledge of the UNHCR *Guidelines on the Protection of Refugee Women* and these guidelines.

The guidelines make sense in the context of UNHCR assisted returns and, certainly, UNHCR staff should be held accountable for their implementation. Greater challenges exist, however, when refugees and IDPs return spontaneously, without international assistance or protection. The majority of refugees in many situations return in just such a manner. There are many reasons that refugees and displaced persons do not take part in formal return programs. These programs are often slow in setting up, often legitimately so because of UNHCR's concerns that conditions are not yet safe enough for return. In the meantime, however, refugees and displaced persons may fear that if they delay return, they will be unable to reclaim their land, find jobs, or take part in political processes unfolding in their home country. Ensuring that returning women and children return in safety in such situations requires the cooperation of host country officials, home country officials, peacekeeping forces, and other actors that may have had minimal previous contact with the uprooted populations. In recognition that spontaneous returns are likely to take place, UNHCR and other humanitarian agencies will need to make sure that all parties, from the refugees to these other actors, are aware of the potential protection problems that returning women and children may face.

Repatriation, Reconstruction, and Assistance for Women

A range of assistance issues is related to return of women. Often, the infra-structures of countries that produce refugees are destroyed during the wars and violence that cause the movements. Refugees (and internally displaced) may return to villages that have no health clinics, roads, schools, food stores, or other basic items. It may be months or years before the communities become self-sustaining. During this period, most of the assistance issues—access to food, access to health care, education, employment—already discussed in the context of displacement continue to be problems.

Much of the earliest analysis of the special repatriation needs of women focused on returns to Afghanistan in event of a Soviet withdrawal. A survey of trained Afghan women conducted in 1988 identified a number of priorities for repatriation that eerily echoes analyses more than a decade later during the second wave of Afghan returns.[12] These included:

- Education—About 70 percent of the women surveyed cited education as a top priority in the reconstruction of Afghanistan. They noted that reconstruction would not be effective if the populace were uneducated. The two most critical needs regarding education were teacher training and expansion of female education.
- Health Care—The women supposed that health care, poor prior to the Soviet invasion, had deteriorated as a result of ten years of war. They noted that the rigors of the return as well as landmine explosions and intergroup conflicts were likely to produce an increased need for health care. Further, they stated that the refugees had become accustomed to a higher level of health care in Pakistan and therefore would have heightened expectations. The educated women argued that it would be wise to take advantage of this situation in order that people, especially women, become more and more accustomed to seeking health assistance when needed.
- Future of Widows, Women with Handicapped Husbands, and Orphans—The traditional social welfare system that existed in Afghanistan had broken down, the women stated. Traditionally, widows were absorbed into the husband's family, sometimes marrying a brother of the husband. In current Afghanistan, however, there would be too many widows for these traditional patterns to work. Many families consist only of women and children. The widows will therefore require special programs including a registration process to identify widows among the refugees, assistance in returning to their homes, assistance in rebuilding their homes, and training programs to prepare them to earn money to support their families.

A major issue facing those planning returns is how to utilize the talents to be found in the refugee camps to help in the reconstruction of their countries. Tapping the resources that women bring to bear in development is essential to this process. Just as women and children are a majority of the refugee and displaced population, they are a majority of the returnees. And, because the events that have skewed the refugee population's demographics (casualties of war) are to be found among the population that remained, a high proportion of those involved overall in reconstruction will be women.

The survey in two provinces in Pakistan cited above demonstrated the diversity of resources that women bring to repatriation but it also showed serious obstacles to their active involvement in reconstruction. The survey sought to identify women in refugee villages and urban areas who have received training in education and health fields; to evaluate the role they may play in repatriation and reconstruction; and to make recommendations on the kinds of programs that should be funded to assist in the rebuilding of Afghanistan.

The survey found that the proportion of Afghan women who had been trained prior to coming to Pakistan was minimal. A larger number of women received training through refugee programs as health workers and traditional birth attendants. Many of these women had, however, received only superficial instruction in basic mother/child health care. Only about 5 percent of the women identified during the survey had received training which could be considered adequate by international standards. Most were teachers with a smaller number being trained medical personnel.

The survey noted an interest on the part of NGOs to upgrade their skills training programs for refugee women. It appeared, however, that the NGOs were not adequately prepared to take on this role. They would need help in designing programs. The authors of the survey recommended that the most skilled women be chosen to serve as trainers, networkers, and supervisors in order to get their expertise disseminated throughout the community.[13]

Several obstacles existed to utilizing fully the resources these skilled women could bring to bear. Many of the women were committed to utilizing their skills but expressed concern about return to Afghanistan, particularly if a fundamentalist government were installed. One woman noted: "our most serious problem will be overcoming the narrow-mindedness of men who want to keep the women at home and will use the Russian invasion as their justification."[14]

According to the survey, the trained women tended to come from only two areas inside Afghanistan—Kabul and Kandahar. Most wanted to return to their former places of residence, although a small number indicated a willingness to go wherever their skills were needed. The latter wanted to organize educated women to supervise outreach programs to educate rural women. One of the side benefits of the refugee situation, it appeared, was to sensitize educated, urban Afghan women to the needs of the rural women. As one woman stated: "I never realized how bad the situation for rural women was until I walked out through the countryside and then worked with women in the refugee villages. It now will be up to the educated women to do something for their rural sisters. Those of us who have medical training are particularly responsible to help them learn to take care of themselves and their children."[15]

At the urgings of educated women associated with all of the political parties, a women's centre was established in Peshawar to serve as an assembly point for women concerned about repatriation. In addition, the centre provided skills training and literacy programs for Afghan women to help a larger cross-section of women be productive on return.

The UNICEF study cited above also noted the need for programs to sensitize male refugees to the need to involve women in repatriation and reconstruction. "During the Inventory process, quite a few supportive men were encountered, including high level resistance party officials. These men have begun to realize that the support of women will be important because of the large number of men who have died, been seriously maimed, or will not return to Afghanistan. . . . Supportive men should be involved in developing and implementing these desensitization programs because, after all, most of them undoubtedly went through the process themselves."[16]

The results of the survey further pointed to the need to think through the requirements of repatriation, from the women's point of view, at the start rather than end of a refugee experience. The study included a number of recommendations for training programs, which, had they been in operation for ten years, would have provided a good base of trained refugee women to help with repatriation and reconstruction.

Afghan reconstruction in the 1990s quickly gave way to internal conflict and the eventual dominance of the Taliban.[17] The restrictions on women's rights made it impossible to carry out most of the plans for women's involvement in rebuilding Afghanistan. Following the overthrow of the Taliban, a second wave of returns have taken place amidst new interest in promoting an effective role for women, as well as continued barriers to their involvement. The Afghan-American Summit on Afghan Recovery and Reconstruction, held at Georgetown University, outlined a number of initiatives, particularly for the Ministry of Women's Affairs, to address the needs and enhance the role of women and girls. Objectives included increasing women's knowledge of their rights; establishing laws that codify family status, inheritance, and property rights for women; updating and revising Afghan legal structures to protect the rights of women; establishing mechanisms to compensate for "educational gaps" resulting from Taliban rule and displacement; increasing women's literacy; increasing women's access to reproductive health care services; establishing services for women traumatized by war, loss, abuse, and neglect; increasing the ability of women to support themselves and their families; and meeting the urgent need for a safer and more secure environment. The summit recognized that the return and reintegration of refugee and displaced women would be a particular challenge for the country, but the participants also recognized that these women would be a resource for the development of Afghanistan, particularly if the skills learned in exile were fully utilized.[18]

Recognizing that communities receiving returnees often need help in reintegrating them, UNHCR has developed a program of "quick impact projects" (QIPs) designed to facilitate return. Used initially in Central America, Cambodia, and Mozambique, these projects have become a mainstay of repatriation efforts. QIPs are not aimed at the immediate survival needs of returnees, nor are they long-term development projects. Rather, they are small-scale projects designed to fill the gap that exists between relief and development. In Nicaragua, for example, QIPs designed with the specific needs and resources of women in mind gave priority to microprojects that benefited women and their families, including nutrition centers, wells, crop and livestock projects, and small scale income generation projects. QIPs generally involve not only the returnees but also the already resident population in order to reduce potential tensions that may arise if only the refugees and displaced persons are assisted.[19]

Lack of economic opportunities on return is one of the most serious assistance and protection issues facing returning women and children. War-torn societies have generally lost their capacity for economic self-support and find it difficult to recover. High rates of unemployment are found throughout these countries. When landmines prevent resumption of agricultural activities, and no urban employment is available, returnees can become desperate. One study conducted by adolescent researchers in Sierra Leone described a too familiar outcome for women and girls: "Some young people interviewed said they had already returned home from Guinea or an IDP camp but were forced to leave again in search of work because of lack of assistance. Some former refugee girls and women said they became involved in commercial sex work for their survival and have traveled to other parts of Sierra Leone to provide services to UNAMSIL troops."[20] Increases in prostitution, including the trafficking of women and girls for the sex trade, has occurred in other postconflict states with large peacekeeping forces.[21]

Reclaiming property is a problem that faces many returning refugees and internally displaced persons. Land may have been seized by government authorities. Other people, sometimes equally in need, may have moved onto the property after the refugees and displaced persons fled. Oftentimes, IDPs live in housing formerly occupied by refugees. Added to the general difficulty are problems faced more specifically by women, particularly widows, in reclaiming property. The UNHCR *Handbook on Voluntary Repatriation* emphasizes the need to take these issues into account in planning and carrying out repatriation programs:

> Special attention needs to be paid to the question of access to land for residential and agricultural use by returnee women heads of households. If the local legislation or traditional practice does not grant returnee women the same rights to land as returnee men, UNHCR has to draw the attention of the authorities to this problem and seek to find suitable ways to rectify the situation. If this is not done early enough, there is a danger that returnee women may lose out in the competition for land, either by not getting access or being evicted. This may in turn lead to increased vulnerability and possible internal displacement. In any case, UNHCR has to closely monitor the handling of returnees' access to land and to ensure, if necessary through intervention, that returnee women have access to land on the same footing as returnee men.[22]

In Burundi, for example, women cannot exercise a legal right to inherit land although there are complicated circumstances when women may be allowed to occupy and work land after the death of a husband or father.[23] Facing a similar legal system at the time of the repatriation to Rwanda, the Ministry for Women's Affairs, UNHCR, and local NGOs spearheaded a successful effort to change the law to give women the right to own property.

Demobilization of combatants is a further issue that affects the protection of refugees and displaced persons in postconflict situations. Many combatants are adolescents who have few skills other than war making. If not given access to alternative economic opportunities, the demobilized soldiers may turn to other violent activities in order to survive. Women and girls who have been involved with military forces, or were themselves drawn into the conflict, face special problems. As one report on adolescents in Sierra Leone described:

> Many women and girls were excluded from formal demobilization as others rushed in for assistance. Had those who spontaneously returned home arrived with weapons, they would have raised suspicions among those who received them. But arriving without them created further barriers to receiving care. Desperate for help, some of these young people left home again to try and get weapons in order to comply. One adolescent girl in Peacock Farm said, " . . . three of my friends have gone back to Kono . . . they said they are going to get weapons and disarm." Others felt they could not go back and approach

commanders for help or to be placed on demobilization lists by them. Instead, they waited for other opportunities that never materialized.[24]

That many of the demobilizing women and girls had been raped only complicated the reintegration process, as it does for many refugee and displaced persons as well. In Sierra Leone, as elsewhere, "rape is often a taboo subject [and] failure to confront the issue perpetuates a culture of silence that exacerbates an already difficult recovery from these crimes. Advocacy and community sensitization work focused on preparing families and communities for their return and creating sympathy for them rather than stigmatization has only scratched the surface of what is needed."[25]

In response to the needs of women in postconflict societies, UNHCR, with the active encouragement of several donor countries, established special women's initiatives. These include the Bosnian, Rwandan, and Kosovo Women's Initiatives. Begun in 1996 after the Dayton Peace Accords with a $5 million budget, the Bosnian Women's Initiative (BWI) supported activities in four areas: psychological support; community services; education; and, in particular, income-generating projects. Under the assumption that putting money into the hands of women facilitates their empowerment, the BWI actively encouraged the formation of women's NGOs. According to an assessment of the women's initiatives, "the total number of direct beneficiaries of BWI was 63,400. The majority of approved projects were income generation activities (73 percent), while 16 percent were related to community services and 11 percent involved educational/vocational training. There were four inter-entity cooperation projects (involving women of different ethnic groups and nationalities) and one countrywide project to publish a women's magazine."[26]

The Rwandan Women's Initiative (RWI) followed in 1997 after the mass return of refugees from Tanzania and Zaire. Originally to be funded at the level of $7 million, RWI actually received less than $5 million in resources. The initiative benefited over 50,000 Rwandan women and girls, targeting widows, women heads of household, genocide survivors, children born of rape, unaccompanied minors, and foster families. It supported literacy and education projects, income generation and skills training, and psychosocial support in women's centers. RWI was overseen by the Rwandan government ministry for women, UNHCR, and an umbrella group of local women's NGOs.[27]

The Kosovo Women's Initiative (KWI) was founded in mid-1999 after the mass return of Kosovars from Albania and Macedonia. More generously funded than the other initiatives at $10 million, the KWI directly benefited 27,000 women in 219 projects. Another 80,000 people benefited directly or indirectly. The initiative was more broadly conceived than its counterparts in Bosnia and Rwanda. The KWI backed projects focused on psychological and social support, clinic-based and community reproductive health education, SGBV, microcredit and income generation, skills training/capacity building of women's groups, and legal assistance. It also had a more explicit protection focus to its activities. It worked through four international NGOs that channeled funds to local women's groups and built their capacity.[28]

All of the women's initiatives were aimed at the empowerment of women in the reconstruction of their countries. The meaning of empowerment was not always clear, however, as an evaluation of the BWI indicated:

> The notion of empowerment has been used in a bewildering variety of ways, from the mundane to the profound, from the particular to the very general. Empowerment is seen to occur at a number of different levels, to cover a range of different dimensions and to materialize through a variety of different processes. However, central to the idea of empowerment is "power." This is the starting point for clarifying the notion of empowerment. One way of thinking about power is in the terms of the ability to make choices: to be disempowered, therefore, implies to be denied choice. The notion of empowerment is thus inescapably bound up with "disempowerment" and refers to the processes by which those who have been denied the ability to make choices acquire such ability. In other words, empowerment entails a process of change.[29]

Ironically, the women's initiatives themselves sometimes failed to involve local women in the planning and implementation of programs. An assessment of the initiatives concluded: "The initiatives varied in how much women beneficiaries were part of the process of owning and planning projects, both in initial consultations and advisory structures. There is heavy top-down involvement at times, with local women added to committees or project review boards seemingly as an afterthought. This is reflected in language sometimes, which hints at women as passive, simply recipients or beneficiaries of projects, or sometimes "the target group."[30] One of the most meaningful contributions of the initiatives, however, was the support given to building and maintaining local women's groups that could support women's initiatives over the long term.

The initiatives highlight the relative balance to be given to women-specific programs and to mainstreaming women's concerns into broader reconstruction activities. There were many advantages to women-specific initiatives, in targeting the specific needs and capacities of women in the return, reintegration and reconstruction process. Mainstream programs too often neglect women's issues. However, targeted programs can raise problems of their own, when they "isolate women, prompt accusations of special treatment for

women, or risk marginalization, an issue that becomes pressing in times of
tight funding."[31] Ensuring the continuation of the women's programs when
support is no longer available from UNHCR or other donors is a pressing issue for all three initiatives.

Maintaining the involvement of women, as well as the services they need
and the talents they can contribute, is a broader problem in postconflict return
situations. Refugee women from El Salvador and Guatemala developed
strong women's associations while in exile. These organizations provided
them with new political skills as well as income generation opportunities. De-
scribing Salvadoran refugees in Honduras, one study found:

> nearly all participated in some way in public life through workshops, commit-
> tees, and other initiatives, becoming laborers, community leaders, and security
> guards. These pursuits in turn enhanced their self-esteem. Equally important, the
> refugee camps offered health care and educational opportunities hitherto un-
> available to most of the rural poor in El Salvador. Virtually all children attended
> school and adult women were able to take literacy classes.[32]

Following repatriation and the peace settlement that ended conflict in El Salvador, the situation reverted to preconflict expectations about women's role:

> Male attitudes about appropriate roles for women again changed, or, more pre-
> cisely, reverted to what they had been prior to war and exile. Living conditions
> did as well. A combination of factors related to poverty and male resistance
> made it all but impossible for the Salvadoran women in returnee settlements to
> make full use of the skills and organizational capacities that they had recently
> acquired. These included unemployment, alcoholism, and violence, which re-
> emerged and then intensified.[33]

Guatemalan refugee women's organizations had been similarly powerful in-
fluences on their members' lives: "Women's organizations were the major ve-
hicles for incorporating women into community life. By the beginning of
1990, such organizations had taken strong root among refugee women in
Mexico. . . . The most prominent of the organizations to mobilize refugee
women was the Organizacion de Mujeres Guatemaltecas (Organization of
Guatemalan Women), popularly known as Mama Maquin, which was formally established in 1990 in Chiapas."[34] Following return, the Guatemalan
refugee women faced situations similar to their Salvadoran sisters. In addition, they found themselves without the social support of other returnees:
"The return movement separated women who had developed strong relations
when they lived in close proximity. Indeed, return brought many of the
refugees to settlements far from their places of origin. Even those who returned to their home communities reported finding strangers there who had

migrated during the conflict; consequently, returnees often lived in communities where the residents did not know each other."[35]

The returning women still found their experiences in exile to be valuable for themselves and their children. The Guatemalan women reported they "have not reverted to former attitudes of subordination and insignificance. They recognize themselves as having special needs and rights and defend these to the best of their abilities, even though doing so is often difficult."[36] The Salvadoran women echoed this sentiment, "They do not willingly accept the small spaces the men expected them to occupy. Further, with regard to education, the women interviewed were adamant about their need for schooling for the girls as well as the boys in their families."[37]

SETTLEMENT IN COUNTRIES OF ASYLUM

In a number of countries, particularly in Africa, refugees have been permitted to remain indefinitely in the country in which they initially sought asylum. Some move into rural settlements; others settle spontaneously in cities. For a period of time, the settled refugees are generally provided international assistance to help them adjust and to minimize their impact on the host countries. Significant local settlement has been seen in the Sudan, Tanzania, Zaire, Costa Rica, Mexico, and elsewhere. However, local integration of refugees appears to be a dwindling option for refugees today. Even countries that previously permitted or even encouraged local settlement are hostile to the notion today. Generally poor countries within even poorer regions, these countries argue that they cannot shoulder the burden of local integration, particularly during an era of reduced international funding.

In rural settlements, many of the assistance issues encountered in camps and upon repatriation also face refugee women and children. Access to schooling and health care are of particular concern, especially after the settlement has ceased to receive international assistance. The refugees may then be reliant on the health care and educational systems of their host country. Refugees in general, and women in particular, may be considered a low priority for services.

The decision to move refugees into settlements can be a controversial one as well. In a number of countries, refugees have wished to remain in border areas, closer to their home country but the host government has wanted to move them to an interior location, often because of security or other reasons. At times, UNHCR has wished to move camps as well, particularly where the safety of the refugees is in question at a border location. Ensuring the participation of refugee women in the decisions about moving into settlements is critical in these situations.

Legal rights are also of concern. A study of rural settlements in Africa found that few refugees were accorded full legal and political rights, even those born in the settlement. In effect, the residents remained refugees in their new homes. Without these rights, they had no capacity to influence political decisions that affected them. Absence of full legal rights also impeded their ability to attain full economic self-support because they could be denied access to markets, ownership of land and businesses, right to travel freely throughout the country, etc. Access to employment and income support for needy families is a further issue affecting refugee women who are settled in countries of asylum.

Spontaneously settled refugees, particularly those living in urban settings, face even further difficulties. Obtaining legal residency is often impossible, particularly where governments are trying to discourage settlement in cities. Even in rural areas, spontaneously settled refugees often do not have identity cards, thereby limiting their access to services.

Refugees who are long-stayers in host countries tend to be younger and disproportionately female. As one study found:

> The Nakivale refugee camp in Uganda, for example, currently accommodates around 15,000 refugees (mainly from Rwanda and the DRC), of whom 10,000 are under the age of 14. In Kenya's Kakuma and Dadaab refugee camps, just over half of the population are aged below 18, while the figure stands at some 58 percent in the older settlements for Burundian refugees in Tanzania. In Algeria, the Tindouf refugee camps "have always been inhabited almost exclusively by vulnerable refugees: women, children, and the elderly. They are almost entirely devoid of adult male population.[38]

These demographics, in combination with the marginalization of many of the settlements, make it difficult for residents to become economically self-sufficient. Refugees tend to be settled in very poor areas of the host country, with inadequate natural resources. Two such settlements are described as follows:

> At the Oruchinga camp for Rwandan refugees in Uganda, for example, one finds that "the land size allocated is inadequate, the soil is not very fertile and there is a lack of fertilisers. This results in low yields, which means that there is not enough produce left over to sell."
>
> In the Kyangwali settlement, which has been described as "one of the few settlements in Uganda that can reasonably claim a high level of self sufficiency," the primarily Congolese refugee population is nevertheless confronted with a range of economic constraints, including geographical isolation, the limited size of the local market, high transportation costs, a lack of information about market conditions, poor terms of trade and the imposition of taxes on economic activities inside the settlement.[39]

The settlement of refugees in countries of asylum has impacts on the residents of the host country as well. Often, those who are most adversely affected by the presence of refugees are the poorest residents. As one report notes, "poorer hosts can lose from competition for food, work, wages, services and common property resources. Vulnerable hosts . . . lack refugees' option of sending their weaker dependents to camps and settlements."[40] Since women and children are often the most vulnerable populations in developing countries, they may be the ones at the greatest disadvantage from the presence of refugees. This issue needs much more attention from those planning assistance programs in refugee situations.

FROM RELIEF AND DEPENDENCY TO DEVELOPMENT: THE ROLE OF WOMEN

Development-oriented humanitarian assistance is emerging as a key option for dealing with the consequences of displacement for the refugees and displaced persons themselves, the countries and communities in which they seek safety, and their countries and communities of origin. Recognizing that long-term care and maintenance is costly both in human and economic terms, there has been interest in exploring new, development-oriented programs for refugees and displaced persons.[41]

During the 1980s, much of the focus of development-oriented programs was on countries of asylum. With little repatriation occurring during that period, the emphasis was on greater self-sufficiency for refugees during their displacement. Development-oriented projects took two major forms. First were small-scale projects that addressed a variety of refugee needs—such as health care, employment, and education—with particular attention paid to enhancing the refugees' capacity for economic self-support. The second were large-scale projects to improve the infrastructure of the host country. With the aim of enhancing the economic independence of refugees in camps and local settlements, as well as easing the burden of refugees on their host country and facilitating return where possible, some of these programs were focused exclusively on refugee participants, while others served refugees and other residents.

Experts argued that to be successful, the development orientation must be put in place at the outset of a refugee emergency in order to warrant against dependency. This approach tends to run counter to the immediate demands of the crisis, however, when most organizations are preoccupied with saving lives. In their book on refugee aid and development, Mary Anderson and Peter Woodrow state some principles of assistance:[42]

- Both relief and development programs should be more concerned with increasing local capacities and reducing vulnerabilities than with providing goods, services, or technical assistance. In fact, goods, services, or technical assistance should be provided only insofar as they support sustainable development by increasing local capacities and reducing local vulnerabilities.
- The way that such resources are transferred must be held to the same test.
- Programming must not be solely preoccupied with meeting urgent physical/material needs, but must integrate such needs into efforts that address the social/organizational and motivational/attitudinal elements of the situation as well.

Development-oriented programs for refugees were believed to hold two major advantages. First, there was a perception that these programs would facilitate durable solutions. With greater capacity to provide for themselves, the refugees would be better prepared to return to their countries of origin if conditions permit, or integrate into the local society if settlement in the country of first asylum or third country were possible.

The second aim was to reduce costs. A large part of the funds used in refugee assistance programs support basic care and maintenance including shelter, food, and clothing. To the extent that refugees are able to integrate into the host country, the cost to the international community will be minimized.

There were major impediments to accomplishing the development goals of refugee assistance, however, that effectively undermined the large-scale use of these approaches. First, many asylum countries were concerned that development-oriented refugee assistance projects would, in fact, result in the de facto integration of refugees into the local society. There was concern that greater independence on the part of refugees would lessen international pressure on the country of origin for voluntary repatriation or on donor countries for contributions to the assistance system. Host countries believed that refugee camps reminded the world community to work toward long-term solutions and to maintain their share of the burden of assisting refugees.

Second, refugees often settled in the poorest areas of their host countries, where local inhabitants also struggled to survive. To complicate matters, sufficient arable land, water, and work opportunities for both the local population and the refugees were often in short supply. In such situations, it was not possible to assist refugees without providing similar opportunities for the local inhabitants. Without satisfactory support for their own citizens, the reluctance of host governments to permit refugee development-oriented activities was to be expected.

Host countries often put two conditions on development-oriented assistance for refugees: (1) equitable burden sharing between the international community and the host country, and (2) additionality of assistance provided to refugees. By equitable burden sharing, the host countries wanted the international community to provide direct assistance to refugees and help the host country in dealing with the negative impacts arising from the presence of the refugees. In this regard, the host countries sought assistance in dealing with impacts on their infrastructures, such as medical care system, roads, water systems, etc. A 1983 report of a Meeting of Experts on Refugee Aid and Development, convened by the UNHCR, noted:

> Host countries and their populations are increasingly affected by large influxes of refugees. . . . Economies and services [are] under severe pressure . . . their own people seriously deprived. . . . [Refugees] place additional burdensome economic and social infrastructures as well as on government administration, and may damage or destroy the environment.[43]

The presence of spontaneously settled refugees was and continues to be of particular concern to host countries. Assistance from the UN system generally goes to refugee camps or settlements where refugees are registered for receiving aid. Spontaneously settled refugees generally do not present themselves for such assistance, living off the local economy instead. As a result, where there are significant numbers of spontaneously settled refugees, it is particularly important to include both refugees and local inhabitants in development programs.

This point leads naturally to the second issue raised by host countries: additionality of refugee development assistance. Host countries generally insist that refugee assistance be over and above the normal development assistance they would receive if there were no refugees in the country. The host countries, in view of their limited resources, do not feel it is equitable to have to share their development aid with refugees or go into debt on their behalf. Donors, on the other hand, point to limited availability of development funds and to the advantages that accrue to host countries from integrating refugees into their regular development plans. Refugees can then contribute to the development of the areas in which they live.

Even where the institutional and financial constraints are overcome, still other factors may influence the potential success of development-oriented approaches to refugee assistance—the state of the local economy, the skill level and educational background of the refugees, their attitude

toward integrating into the host country, and the existence of viable program ideas.

A further factor that has complicated efforts to promote development approaches in countries of asylum is the demographic composition of the
refugee population. Many of the projects designed to promote development—
particularly large road projects and reforestation schemes—are geared toward
men. Since women and children make up the majority of the world's refugee
population, a failure to take into account these demographics can adversely
affect the success of development efforts. On the other hand, women are an
important resource for development and can contribute greatly to building
self-reliance for their communities. New approaches and new institutional
arrangements may well be needed, however, if their contributions are to be
felt.

Whereas the limits of the development approach in countries of asylum
have restricted its application, the large-scale repatriations and returns of
refugees and internally displaced persons gave it new life in the 1990s,
though still with many barriers. Experts began speaking of the transition from
relief through reconstruction to development as a necessary progression in
postconflict societies. UNHCR also recognized that the needs of returnees
would be beyond its own mandate and capacities for assistance. As the *Handbook on Voluntary Repatriation* states:

> Material destruction and absence of development activities compounded by hid-
> den anti-personnel mines on roads and pathways, around public utilities, ran-
> domly spread in villages and widely dispersed in agricultural, pasture and forest
> lands make any reintegration in safety and with dignity a dire task, beyond the
> mandate and resources of UNHCR alone. In fact, the general material conditions
> that refugees will encounter upon return may be worse than when they left. Thus
> reintegration should be addressed with the twin strategy of, on the one hand,
> meeting the most urgent livelihood and community rehabilitation needs and on
> the other establishing and/or reinforcing complementary, collaborative links
> with developmental actors.[44]

Incorporating refugee populations into development projects requires that
institutions that traditionally have had responsibility for development programs take on new roles vis-à-vis refugees. Until the past decade, almost all
international assistance to refugees was administered through the UNHCR.
Development-oriented agencies, such as the UN Development Program
(UNDP), have had only limited relationship to refugee issues. With the new
focus on development, however, such organizations as the UNDP, the World
Bank, and the International Monetary Fund are also becoming involved. Private organizations that have expertise and experience in implementing

women and development projects are also playing a more active role in refugee programming.

CONCLUSION

Finding durable solutions to refugee situations is a major challenge of the international community. The consequences of failure to find these solutions are considerable for the refugees, the host country, the country of origin, and the international community itself. Refugee women must be an integral part of all efforts to find solutions if these are to be successful.

NOTES

Full citations can be found in the select bibliography.

1. Tessa Williams and Jeff Crisp, "Namibia Together Again," *Refugees* 79 (1989): 24.

2. Reported by delegations of the Women's Commission for Refugee Women and Children to the Thai-Cambodian border, Malawi, and Pakistan.

3. Gunilla Wingo, *Female Attitudes and Social Well-Being: Preparing for Repatriation; A Pilot Study in Two Afghan Refugee Villages in Baluchistan* (Quetta: UNHCR and Radd Barnen/Swedish Save the Children, 1990), 4.

4. Beatrice Manz, *Refugees of a Hidden War: The Aftermath of Counterinsurgency in Guatemala* (Albany: State University of New York Press, 1987).

5. United Nations High Commissioner for Refugees (UNHCR), *Handbook on Voluntary Repatriation: International Protection* (Geneva: UNHCR, 1996).

6. Global Consultations on International Protection: Report of the Meetings within the Framework of the Standing Committee (Third Track), Report of the Fourth Meeting in the Third Track (May 22–24, 2002) A/AC.96/961 (2002), 31.

7. UNHCR, *Handbook on Voluntary Repatriation*.

8. Women's Commission for Refugee Women and Children, *Rights, Reconstruction and Enduring Peace: Afghan Women and Children after the Taliban* (New York: Women's Commission for Refugee Women and Children, December 2001).

9. Women's Commission for Refugee Women and Children, *Report of Delegation to Hong Kong*, 22

10. Women's Commission, *Report of Delegation to Hong Kong*, 22.

11. UNHCR, *Handbook on Voluntary Repatriation*.

12. Kerry M. Connor, *Skill Inventory of Afghan Women Refugees in the North West Frontier and Baluchistan Provinces* (Islamabad: UNICEF, December 1988).

13. Connor, 5.

14. Connor, 31.

15. Connor, 26.

16. Connor, 39–40.

17. See Julie A. Mertus, *War's Offensive on Women: The Humanitarian Challenge in Bosnia, Kosovo, and Afghanistan* (Bloomfield, Conn.: Kumarian Press, 2000) for discussion of women under the Taliban.

18. Susan Forbes Martin, Patricia Weiss-Fagen, Lydia Mann-Bondat, and Katherine Leggett Stone, "Women, Families and Society," in Afghanistan-American Summit on Recovery and Reconstruction, *Afghanistan: Looking toward the Future* (Washington, D.C.: Georgetown University, 2002).

19. Susan Forbes Martin, "Return and Reintegration: The Experiences of Refugee and Displaced Women," in Barry Stein, Frederick Cuny, and Pat Reed, *Refugee Repatriation during Conflict: A New Conventional Wisdom* (Dallas, Tex.: The Center for the Study of Societies in Crisis, 1995).

20. Women's Commission for Refugee Women and Children, *Precious Resources: Participatory Research Study with Adolescents and Youth in Sierra Leone* (New York: Women's Commission for Refugee Women and Children, April–July 2002).

21. See for example, Chris Corren, *Gender Audit of Reconstruction Programmes in South Eastern Europe* (Urgent Action Fund and Women's Commission for Refugee Women and Children, June 2000).

22. UNHCR, *Handbook on Voluntary Repatriation*.

23. Women's Commission, *Out of Sight, Out of Mind*.

24. Women's Commission, *Precious Resources*.

25. Women's Commission, *Precious Resources*.

26. Women's Commission, *UNHCR Policy*, 80.

27. Women's Commission, *UNHCR Policy*, 81.

28. Women's Commission, *UNHCR Policy*, 82.

29. Naila Kabeer, *The Conditions and Consequences of Choice: Reflections on the Measurement of Empowerment* (Geneva: UNRISD, 1999), 2, as reported in Women's Commission, *UNHCR Policy*.

30. Women's Commission, *UNHCR Policy*.

31. Women's Commission, *UNHCR Policy*.

32. Patricia Weiss-Fagen, "Refugee Women in El Salvador and Guatemala: Challenges and Lessons of Reintegration," for the International Center for Research on Women (April 2000).

33. Fagen, "Refugee Women."

34. Fagen, "Refugee Women."

35. Fagen, "Refugee Women."

36. Fagen, "Refugee Women."

37. Fagen, "Refugee Women."

38. Jeff Crisp, "No solutions in sight: the problem of protracted refugee situations in Africa," UNHCR Working Paper No. 75 (January 2003).

39. Crisp, "No solutions."

40. Robert Chambers, "Hidden Losers? The Impact of Rural Refugees and Refugee Programs on Poorer Hosts," *International Migration Review* 20, no. 2 (Summer 1986): 245.

41. See, for example, Steven Holtzman, "Rethinking 'Relief' and 'Development' in Transitions from Conflict," prepared for the Brookings Initiative on Relief and Development, January 1999.

42. Anderson and Woodrow, *Rising from the Ashes*, 97.

43. "Refugee Aid and Development," Executive Committee, Thirty-fourth Session (AIAC, 96/627, contains report of the meeting of experts, September 12, 1983).

44. UNHCR, *Handbook on Voluntary Repatriation*.

Resettled Laotian Refugees in New Zealand. (UNHCR/S. Pintus)

7

Refugee Women in Industrialized Countries

I became a citizen last year; I am now an American. . . . For some refugees, becoming an American is not an easy thing to do. It means giving up that final thing that is yours, your nationality. . . . When I took my oath, I thought, "Oh my God! Everything is gone!" But after it happened, I never thought about it. The most painful part was just thinking about it. There is something exciting about holding my new blue passport and knowing that I will vote next year for the president.[1]

Refugee women come to industrialized countries in two ways. Some are resettled from countries of first asylum and enter through formal admission programs. Others are direct arrivals who come spontaneously to industrialized countries and then request asylum.

Resettlement in third countries is generally considered to be the least desirable solution for refugees because it moves them far from their own countries and cultures. In many situations, however, resettlement is the best solution for the individuals and groups involved, particularly when needed to provide protection or durable solutions for refugees. Their country of asylum may be unwilling or unable to allow the refugees to remain indefinitely; return to the country of origin may be impossible for the foreseeable future. As the UNHCR *Handbook on Resettlement* states:

Resettlement is a vital instrument of protection and durable solution. Resettlement under UNHCR auspices is geared primarily to the special needs of refugees under the Office's mandate whose life, liberty, safety, health or other fundamental human rights are at risk in the country where they sought refuge. It is also considered a durable solution, in particular circumstances, for refugees who do not have immediate protection concerns. The decision to resettle a

Table 7.1.   Resettlement Arrivals, 2000–2001

Country	2000	2001
United States**	72,500	68,430
Canada	13,520	12,250
Australia	7,880	6,450
Norway	1,480	1,270
Sweden	1,500	1,090
Finland	760	740
New Zealand	700	760
Denmark	460	530
Netherlands	200	630
Japan	140	40
Ireland	40	50
Iceland	20	20
Total	**99,220**	**92,260**

**Including Family Reunion.
Source: UNHCR *Statistical Yearbook,* 2001.

refugee is normally taken, with priority, when there is no alternative way to guarantee the legal or physical security of the person concerned. In light of this, the common description of resettlement as a "last resort" should not be interpreted to mean that there is a hierarchy of solutions and that resettlement is the least valuable or needed among them. For many refugees, resettlement is, in fact, the best—or perhaps, only—alternative.[2]

Refugees come directly to industrialized countries for a variety of reasons. Escape to North America or Europe may be easier, less dangerous, and more direct for some, for example via airplanes, than is flight to a neighboring country. The refugees may be unwilling or unable to wait in countries of first asylum, afraid for themselves or their families. They may have spouses or other relatives already in the industrialized country whom they are seeking to join more quickly than the formal admissions programs allow. Or, their family members may not have a status in the industrialized country that permits them to reunify through regular channels with their relatives still in the country of origin. The legal processes and problems encountered by women in applying for asylum are discussed in chapter 3.

UNHCR estimates that in 2001 more than 90,000 refugees arrived in industrialized countries (see table 7.1). The United States, Canada, and Australia are the principal destination countries. Countries of origin with significant numbers of resettled refugees included Sudan, Somalia, Iraq, Iran, and Afghanistan. Following the September 11 terrorist attacks, resettlement has declined precipitously, particularly to the United States. In the U.S. fiscal year 2002, fewer than 30,000 refugees were resettled. The countries of origin of resettled refugees included states that were sponsors of terrorists, calling into question the adequacy of mechanisms to screen out those who might pose a security risk. New security provisions were put into place that substantially increased the time and resources necessary for processing applications. Since many of the refugees available for processing were in countries neighboring the terrorist states, concerns also arose as to the safety of U.S. personnel undertaking the screenings. As of April 2003, the pace of resettlement had not yet picked up significantly, leaving many qualified refugees in camps or other vulnerable locations waiting processing of their applications.

Most of the refugee women and children who are resettled in third countries enter as part of a complete family unit. Among some refugee populations, however, a significant number of women-headed households have been resettled. Special efforts have been made to find resettlement opportunities for women who are particularly at risk in countries of first asylum. These include single women as well as victims of rape and torture.

All refugees in industrialized countries, regardless of their family composition, face adjustment problems. These problems can be particularly acute where the culture of the home country and the new country are markedly different. Most resettled refugees are faced with the need to learn a new language. They must also find and maintain employment. Refugees coming from rural areas find it particularly challenging to adapt to urban, industrialized economies and societies.

For refugee women, such an adjustment may be particularly difficult. Yet, resettled women have also shown themselves to be strong resources for the development of their own ethnic communities and their new societies. This chapter explores both the needs and opportunities that the resettlement of refugee women provides.

Admission to Industrialized Countries

Refugee women come to industrialized countries either through resettlement programs or as asylum seekers. Both routes carry pitfalls for refugee women.

Asylum seekers generally enter without prior approval of the new country, which then determines whether the asylum seeker can remain and in what capacity. Signatories to the 1951 UN Convention Relating to the Status of Refugees agree that they will not deport refugees to a country where their life or liberty would be threatened. A grant of asylum does not necessarily mean, however, that the person granted the status will be able to stay permanently in that country. A first step toward finding permanent refuge, however, is to demonstrate that one meets the refugee definition. Chapter 3 examined the problems faced by refugee women during the refugee determination process.

Resettlement decisions are made by governments, often in consultation with UNHCR. Governments have no obligations to take in refugees from abroad. They have complete discretion in determining whether or not they will accept refugees for resettlement. However, a number of countries, including the United States, Canada, Australia, New Zealand, and many European countries, offer resettlement quotas on a yearly basis.

Typically, governments set admission levels and priorities at the start of the year. Most countries establish family reunification as a key purpose of their refugee resettlement and immigration programs. In addition, governments offer resettlement to individuals who are of special interest, either to individuals who have a close personal relationship to the resettlement country (for example, having worked for one of their institutions or having gone to school there) and/or to individuals from countries in which the resettlement country has a special interest (for example, a former colony or ally in a conflict). Finally, resettlement slots are often provided to refugees who are under threat of return to their countries of origin or whose protection is otherwise dependent on resettlement. Several countries also run specialized programs for individuals with special needs: disabled, unaccompanied minors, and, as discussed below, women at risk.

Applicants for resettlement generally must demonstrate that they are refugees under international and/or national law. In addition, they are required to meet other admissions standards—for example, they may need to demonstrate that they are likely to be able to adjust to the new culture. Considerations taken into account include knowledge of the resettlement country's language, skill levels, family members already in the resettlement country, and willingness of the concerned governments or private agencies or groups to sponsor the new arrival.

Among the refugees that UNHCR believes are in desperate need of resettlement are women who may not otherwise fit the resettlement countries' criteria for admission. These women have generally experienced severe trauma and are living in circumstances in which their traditional support systems have broken down. Yet, they may have no relatives in a third country, no knowledge of the language or transferable skills, and may demonstrate a level of need that makes private groups unwilling to risk sponsorship, which requires a financial commitment.

In response to the difficulties faced by women at risk, UNHCR has identified the need for special "Women at Risk" programs for the admission of refugee women who face specific protection problems. According to the UNHCR *Resettlement Handbook*, "When, despite all possible efforts, it is unlikely that the particular protection problems or related needs of a refugee woman can be adequately addressed in the country of refuge, resettlement should be actively considered."[3] More specifically, the *Handbook* states: "In some instances resettlement may be the preferred and often only solution. This could be the case when women have been raped and when in their society and in their country of refuge a survivor of rape is ostracized. Such a situation could be aggravated when the refugee woman gives birth to a child conceived through rape. In addition to the possible serious consequences of a rape on her physical and mental health, the refugee woman may suffer lifelong rejection by her own family and community."[4]

UNHCR identifies women at risk as:

> For purposes of resettlement, UNHCR considers as women-at-risk those women who have protection problems, and are single heads of families or are accompanied by an adult male who is unable to support and assume the role of the head of the family. They may suffer from a wide range of problems including expulsion, *refoulement* and other security threats, sexual harassment, violence, abuse, torture and different forms of exploitation. Additional problems such women face could derive from persecution as well as from particular hardships sustained either in their country of origin, during their flight or in their country of asylum. The trauma of having been uprooted, deprived of normal family and community support or cultural ties, the abrupt change in roles and status, in addition to the absence of an adult male head of family, renders some women, under certain circumstances, more vulnerable than others.[5]

Some countries have established specific women at risk programs—for example, Canada, Australia, and New Zealand. Such other resettlement countries as the United States grant resettlement to refugee women at risk under the normal processing modalities. UNHCR also encourages special programs to help the resettled women adjust to their new lives, programs that address some of the special needs that the women at risk may have.

Canada's program has been operating the longest and provides the clearest picture of the elements of the special provisions. The original guidelines of the program specified "certain relaxation in admissibility criteria," stating that "the greater the need for protection, the lower the threshold which the applicant should have to meet in terms of potential for successful establishment in Canada."[6]

> Women of first priority were those identified overseas as having specific protection needs in refugee camps, were being harassed by local authorities outside their country, or were in danger of being returned (*refouled*) to their home country. Of second priority were women not in "immediate peril" but whose low skills level, dependent children and other factors meant that they had been passed over by Canada or by other resettlement countries in the past.[7]

At present, women at risk are defined as: "women without the normal protection of a family who find themselves in precarious situations and whose safety is in jeopardy in countries of first asylum. Urgent need of protection or vulnerable cases are given priority. However, women-at-risk may also be women who are not in immediate danger, but who are living in unstable conditions and for whom resettlement in a third country offers the only solution."[8] As of 2002, Canada has admitted more than 2,250 women and children under this program.[9]

NEEDS OF REFUGEE WOMEN IN INDUSTRIALIZED COUNTRIES

Refugee women who are resettled in industrialized countries do not fit a single profile. They come from a variety of countries, and they have had different educational and employment experiences. Few are familiar on arrival with the language or customs of the new country. A minority, however, enters with substantial previous education and skills.

Adjustment to the new culture is a difficult process for many refugee women. Barriers to successful adjustment include those within the host society as well as individual or personal ones. Among the former are racial intolerance and sexual and cultural discrimination aimed against refugee women. Many refugees are of a different race from the majority of the population of their new country. As women, they may face the dual problem of racism and sexism in seeking employment, training or otherwise participating in the activities of the new country.

A further societal factor in adjustment is legal status. The refugees' legal status is an important factor influencing the ease with which she will be able to adjust. Refugees who have been resettled from overseas are legally in the country upon arrival and generally enjoy all legal rights of other residents. Asylum seekers are generally in a more insecure position while they await their hearings. They may be ineligible to seek employment or receive services. The procedure may be protracted, leaving them in limbo for long periods of time. Not knowing if they will be able to remain permanently, asylum seekers may not actively seek out adjustment services.

Personal barriers include family conflicts, traumas suffered during flight, illiteracy, lack of language skills, or religious constraints. Changes in family roles often accompany resettlement. Some families have experienced long periods of separation. Male roles may change drastically in the new society. If their skills are not readily transferable to industrialized countries (for example, agricultural skills), the men may find themselves unable to support their families:

Men often feel neglected and disappointed, which sometimes brings out pa-
triarchal habits and efforts to re-establish traditional roles—even by force if
necessary. In a situation where men are unsure of themselves, they often become skeptical about their wives. Their own feelings of inferiority can lead
to their doubting the love or trustworthiness of their wives. When men
mistrust their wives, they may restrict them and try to control them in an effort to boost their egos.[10]

Intergenerational problems are not uncommon within refugee families.
Children become adjusted to the new society more rapidly than their parents.
They must often act as a bridge between their parents and the new culture, as-
suming a role that in many traditional societies is unknown. Tensions between
parent and child can then develop, with many refugee women feeling inadequate and unable to function in the new environment. Older refugee women
may be particularly susceptible to feelings of isolation caused by these intergenerational tensions. A seventy-year-old Vietnamese woman stated, "How
pitiful I am! I came here in 1975 with my daughter's family. I live with my
daughter, son-in-law and grandchildren but I feel lonely. None of the kids
likes to be near me because grandmom and grandchildren don't understand
each other."[11]

The change in family roles is often accompanied by the loss of traditional
support systems for women:

> Exile frequently entails the loss of traditional support systems upon which a
> woman refugee would normally rely. The absence of friends and extended fam-
> ily can be exceedingly painful. It may also disrupt the way the woman is accus-
> tomed to organizing her life. For example, a woman who has previously relied
> upon family members to care for her children while she is otherwise occupied
> may find that without this support her opportunities in the resettlement country
> considerably diminish.
>
> The loss of neighbours and friends can also limit a woman's possibilities. It
> is not uncommon for refugees to come from closely knit communities where
> neighbours provided both friendship and needed assistance. The loss of these in-
> timate relationships is difficult for women refugees, particularly when they are
> resettled in a community with a more impersonal concept of neighborhood.[12]

The traumatic experiences that many refugee women have had further affect their coping ability in a new culture. Some refugee women, as we have
seen in chapter 3, have been raped, tortured, and sexually abused. They may
have experienced the violent deaths of family members. Having had these
experiences, refugee women may suffer from post-traumatic stress disorder.
In common with refugees in camps, resettled refugees may suffer from depression, anxiety, intrusive thoughts, disassociation or psychic numbing,

hyperalertness, and sleeping and eating disorders. Surveys examining the mental health needs of refugees in the United States have found that single heads of household, widows, and single women are particularly at risk.[13]

Language is a formidable barrier experienced by refugee women when they first enter industrialized countries. Most do not speak the language of their adopted countries upon arrival. A large household survey of Southeast Asian refugees resettled in the United States during the early 1980s showed, for example, that 64 percent of new arrivals spoke no English at the time of entry into the United States, with women having significantly less English skills than men.[14] A survey of more recent refugees to the United States, now largely from eastern Europe, the former Soviet Union, and Africa, showed that 63 percent claimed to speak no English at the time of arrival, with another 27 percent saying they did not speak the language well. By the time of the survey, up to five years after arrival, only 8 percent said they spoke no English. Almost 68 percent claimed to speak English well or fluently.

Industrialized countries generally provide language training for refugees at no cost to the individual. The mechanisms for providing language instruction differ from one country to another. Australia and Canada tend to provide financial support for language training to all newcomers, refugees included. The United States provides special funding for English instruction for refugees only. Classes may be offered through the regular school system or in community-based organizations.

Language instruction has shown itself to be an effective means of language acquisition. A survey in the United States compared English language acquisition among those enrolled in full-time classes, those who combined classes and employment; those working and not enrolled in classes; and those participating in neither jobs nor classes. At the end of six months, the gains in English displayed by those in full-time instruction were significantly greater than those in employment, who progressed more than those who were in neither.[15]

Access to language instruction has been shown to vary by gender, with women enrolling in classes at a lower rate than men. Younger refugees are also more likely to receive training, with refugees who are over the age of fifty being the least likely to be enrolled. Older women are clearly the least likely to receive language instruction of all categories of refugees.[16]

Homebound women are particularly at risk for acquisition of the new language. For those who remain at home, learning the language will be a prime problem since they will have little opportunity to use it.

Barriers to women's access to language training include cultural constraints on women attending classes or otherwise participating in activities that take place outside the house. Practical problems, such as the need for day care and transportation, also impede the ability of women who want to enroll in classes to attend them. The design of some language training programs is at fault as well. Programs may be geared toward very academic study when the women have had no previous education and require survival skills as at least a first step in adjusting to the new culture. Or, class hours may conflict with household or work demands.

These barriers affect access to other forms of education as well. A study of education programs for refugee women states:

> Refugee women enter education programs in the country of resettlement at a severe disadvantage. The vast majority have been excluded from educational experiences at home by a combination of factors: cultural, religious, social and legal customs and gender stereotyping.[17]

A study of the education of refugee women in Britain described the education system as highly structured according to age groups and formal entry routes.

> It lacks flexibility towards foreign qualifications and non-English speaking students. . . . Nowhere in Britain are there enough nursery places available to meet existing demand. Refugee families are expected to compete for the few facilities available. However, the cost of childcare is out of the reach of most refugee families, and the state provision is too selective and competitive to benefit them in any significant way. . . . Another problem is the frequent clash between college hours and children's school hours, making getting children to and from school impossible, thus excluding many women from study.[18]

Failure to learn the new language reduces the ability of refugee women to cope with the new society. A survey in Australia found that refugee women felt that acquisition of English was a prerequisite for active involvement in other aspects of Australian life.[19] In most industrialized countries, some conversance with the new language is necessary for employment. Knowledge of the language also helps women better understand their rights and the benefits to which they may be entitled.

Problems in language acquisition often leads to isolation, with refugee women becoming housebound and dependent on their husbands and children. A study in Denmark described a typical case:

> Presently Ms. S. is isolated at home, occupied with the care of the baby, while her husband attends a vocational training course, being away for the most part of the day. She has no Sri Lankan or Danish friends. . . . Since she does not attend the Danish Refugee Council (DRC) language school, she is not only prevented from learning the Danish language, but is also cut off from contact with other refugees in and outside of the classroom, e.g., at social gatherings arranged by the Danish Refugee Council staff. She has no opportunities of

obtaining relevant information which could help her out of her isolation, e.g., regarding special language classes for mothers with young children.[20]

Employment is a second area affecting the adjustment and integration of refugee women. In most industrialized countries, the labor force participation of women has become very common. Most families require two household incomes. Refugee families find the same phenomenon. One study in the United States found, for example, that refugee families had great difficulty in becoming economically self-sufficient unless there were multiple wage earners in the household.[21]

Experiences differ by country, age, and previous education as to the extent of employment among refugee women. Studies in the United States in the 1980s, of primarily Southeast Asian refugees, found relatively low levels of labor force participation but high levels of employment among refugee women who do enter the labor force.[22] That is, relatively low numbers of refugee women seek outside employment but those who seek jobs tend to become employed. A study in Norway found similar patterns among women from Yugoslavia but showed a lower employment rate among Chilean refugee women. The study showed high levels of what was referred to as "hidden unemployment" among all groups.[23] More recent surveys of refugee women in the United States showed them having higher labor force participation rates (65.3 percent) than the overall U.S. average for women (60.2 percent). They also had lower unemployment rates (3.8 percent versus 4.1 percent). These rates varied greatly by region of origin, however, with labor force participation much higher for women from Eastern Europe and Vietnam than from other parts of Southeast Asia, the former Soviet Union or Africa. Similarly, unemployment ranged from less than one percent for Eastern European refugee women to more than 11 percent for refugee women from the former Soviet Union.[24]

Barriers to seeking and obtaining employment are similar to those discussed regarding language training. First, cultural constraints can be formidable. For refugee women from many developing countries, outside employment may mean a radical change in lifestyle. The women may be working outside of their home for the first time. This may in turn lead to changes in spousal relationships. Further, husbands may be frustrated by their inability to provide sufficiently for their families. Even refugee women from other industrialized societies who were themselves employed at home may see employment in their new country as culturally different from their previous experience.

The need for childcare services is acute among many resettled women who wish to work. Lack of childcare impedes access to job services as well as employment. Childcare concerns are often cited as limitations on employment in surveys asking why refugees were not looking for employment.[25] In some cases, there are long waiting lists for available day care spaces. Often, refugee families are reluctant to use mainstream day care facilities. The Danish study referred to above described one woman's dilemma:

> Mrs. S. is hesitant about leaving the baby in a Danish nursery, having in fact turned down an offer of a nursery place when the baby was three months old. She worries that the culturally alien environment, the Danish teachers, the different methods of child-care and feeding, and the Danish children, will not understand the baby's needs.

When refugee women are employed, families use a wide variety of childcare mechanisms. While some families use formal day care programs, others have relatives and friends care for their children. Many families work a staggered work schedule, with one parent looking after the children while the other works.

A further impediment to employment relates to women who have skills and prior education and/or work experience. They may have difficulty in applying their educational background and working experience in a new setting. The Danish study described these problems:

- insufficient knowledge of qualifications required in Denmark, primarily of Danish language and cultural codes (general as well as in specific branches of professions and general labor market);
- cultural difference, e.g., between educational systems, ways of learning and attitudes toward work, differences between formal and informal learning systems. In Denmark the educational system and labor market is characterized by a high degree of formalization, in contrast to the situation in most of the refugees' homelands;
- physical and technological differences between the Danish production system and labor market and those of the refugees, which make many of the refugees' job categories meaningless in a Danish context.

Underemployment may be the result of difficulties in transforming prior education and skills into the current labor market. As the Norwegian study referenced above noted:

> the average Chilean woman in our study is young, well-educated and urban in orientation. Although the occupational profile is similar to that of the Norwegian female population, the Chilean woman tends to end up in jobs considerably below her occupational and educational background. The Chilean woman who

does work, does so full time in a low income job she dislikes. . . . As a result many have low family incomes and poor standards of living.[26]

Finding safe and affordable housing is a problem facing almost all refugees. Scandinavian countries and the Netherlands have good records of providing subsidized housing for refugees, but most countries either use private housing or a combination of public and private accommodations for new arrivals. Use of public housing can have its drawbacks. Where there are long waiting lists, citizens may express hostility toward refugees who are moved to the head of the line. Public housing in some countries may also be dilapidated and dangerous. One Cuban exile in the United States reported:

My parents live in low-income housing in the middle of a poor . . . neighborhood. My parents do not go for walks. It is nothing short of outrageous to me that the government would place weak, old people in environments where they will meet with hostility. It shows an appalling degree of cultural insensitivity. To my parents, and to other old people in their situation, this is yet one more example of their helplessness and one further bizarre trait of this strange land.[27]

Refugees may not be able to afford to rent better-kept apartments, particularly those in safer neighborhoods.

The new environment may be so frightening as to make even life in a refugee camp seem good in comparison: "I visit Chantha at 183rd Street in the Bronx, a tough neighborhood by any standards and certainly different than anything she has ever known. At times we laugh about times in Khao-I-Dang as though they were the good old days."[28]

Another problem that impedes successful adjustment to the new society is the health status of refugee women. They often arrive with preexisting conditions that are related to their refugee experience. Aside from the physical results of torture and abuse, they may have suffered from long bouts of malnutrition, physical exhaustion from the trek to a country of first asylum, repeated occurrences of malaria or other diseases, and the effects of parasites. In addition, many refugee women have had multiple pregnancies, with one following so soon after another that the health of the mother is jeopardized.

Once in the industrialized country, access to necessary health care may be a problem. In some countries, the issue is financial. Health care is not provided universally to the residents of the country and refugee families may not have sufficient resources to pay for medical services. In the United States, for example, many entry-level jobs pay no health insurance costs. Many of the working poor are ineligible for publicly funded medical insurance. Refugees, like many nationals, may be unwilling to take employment for fear of losing this public benefit.

Even where no financial barriers to health care exist, other impediments stand in the way of effective use of available resources. Health facilities may have inadequate translation and interpretation capacity. Refugees report their reliance on their children to serve as translators. Yet, it is very difficult for refugee women to discuss their medical problems, particularly gynecological ones, through their children.

The services themselves may be seen as inappropriate from the refugee point of view. In many refugee cultures, for example, the Western concept of mental health therapy does not exist. Even where needed, the refugees may be reluctant to utilize the services unless efforts are made to make them more understandable and culturally accessible.

Even death can be an adjustment issue for refugees. In a study of older refugees in the United States, a sixty-four-year-old Vietnamese woman who has had heart problems said that now and then her thoughts turn to death. Although it holds no terror for her, the prospect of being buried in the cemetery next to Americans with no fellow Vietnamese nearby makes her uneasy. She says:

> I am not afraid to die. But I would like to have enough money to be buried in the Vietnamese Senior Citizens cemetery. I would feel comfortable there. If I were buried elsewhere, I would not be able to talk with Americans next to me because I do not speak English.[29]

HELPING REFUGEE WOMEN IN THEIR ADJUSTMENT

> I never realized how strong I am. I always thought I was dependent on others. Now I know I can manage on my own. I feel strong deep inside. I want to encourage other refugee women to know that they can find confidence and hope.[30]

A theme that runs consistently through successful programs for refugee women is empowerment. Refugee women in industrialized countries, no less than those still in camps, must participate in the design and implementation of programs aimed at adaptation and integration into their new societies. Refugee women have shown by their very survival that they are resilient. Even more important, they have much to offer to their new countries.

A newsletter produced by Refugee Women in Development (RefWID— which is a refugee-women run organization) in seven different languages explains the importance of empowerment to its refugee audience:

> When we talk about equal opportunity for women we mean empowering them to employ their capabilities and talents, to contribute to their families' betterment and that of the world, and to make decisions about their own lives. While

all human beings are fundamentally born equal, socio-economic conditions, gender, and other factors divide them into groups of privileged and underprivileged citizens. Gender discrimination is indefensible both on moral and practical grounds as witnessed by the participation of women in many societies throughout history.[31]

Empowerment of refugee women has been promoted in a number of different ways in industrialized countries.

One mechanism builds relationships between refugee women and other women in the community. Le Comite' Intermouvements aupres des Evacues (CIMADE) and the Groupe d'Accueil et Solidarite (GAS) sponsored a meeting at which refugee women from various countries were invited to share their experiences in their home country and in France. The goal was to identify the specific problems of women refugees. As a participant noted,

> Further dialogues followed which were fruitful, as French women and refugee women listened to each other's experiences and forged links. During this time, we reflected on the future of our group and decided to become an autonomous association. For us, the designation "association" means we are in solidarity with each other. We express our feelings; we question ourselves about our own problems; and we understand and feel ourselves to be united by what we have in common.[32]

A similar meeting was held in the United States in 1990 at which refugee women and U.S.-born women compared their experiences. The refugees were surprised to learn that some of their frustrations with life in the United States—particularly dealing with discrimination, the problems of juggling both work and household responsibilities, and the reluctance of male members of their families to share in home responsibilities—were shared by American women. The American women gained a better understanding of the special barriers faced by the refugee women.

A second strategy utilizes refugee self-help groups composed of women. The Refugee Women's Network (RWN) is a national association in the United States whose aim is to "ensure that the unique needs of refugee women are addressed and met through effective advocacy and a strong diverse network of refugee women leaders in the U.S. and overseas." RWN has trained more than 1,000 refugee women in 27 U.S. communities to develop leadership skills that can be used to help their communities. The training includes segments on team building, communication skills, managing change, domestic violence, cultural diversity, coalition building, community analysis, action planning, and conflict and peacemaking. Further technical assistance is offered on such issues as conflict resolution, board development, fundraising, grant writing, programs management, grassroots community organizing, participation in civil society, effective communication, strategic planning, and others. RWN also began a microenterprise project in Atlanta, with the aim of assisting immigrant and refugee women in starting small businesses to contribute to the economy of the family.

Local programs have been started for refugee women as well. The Women's Association of Hmong and Lao, Inc., in Minnesota, is run by and for refugee women. It was founded in 1981 to serve refugee women and their families and to strengthen the relationship among Hmong, Lao, and American women. Through literacy classes, ethnic meals, support groups, socialization activities, and information/referral services, WAHL helps reduce the isolation of refugee women. It also assists them in gaining access to community resources and services. WAHL has a special program for elderly refugees to help their adjustment to the United States. Similarly, Refugee Women's Alliance in Seattle was founded in 1985 to support refugee and immigrant women and their families. The agency was first established by a group of successfully resettled refugee women who sought to provide newly arrived refugee women and children with services not offered by other social service programs. Originally focused on Southeast Asian refugees, the organization now serves families from Ethiopia, Eritrea, Somalia, Russia, the Ukraine, and Eastern Europe as well.

Language training for homebound women takes a number of forms. Tutors sometimes come directly to the homes of women who are unable or fearful of leaving their apartments. Other programs utilize community centers which also provide child care. These centers are often located within walking distance of the refugees' homes and therefore facilitate their attendance. One program has provided workshops at a local center that address health, education, and cultural topics, including an introduction to the new country's educational system so mothers will understand the experiences of their children. Courses are also given in crime prevention.[33]

Other programs have focused on skills training for refugee women to help them obtain employment. The U.S. government, for example, funded a number of projects under the heading of "Multiple Wage Earner" programs designed to help more than one member of a family obtain employment. Most of the projects offered childcare and transportation in addition to the training. The training generally built on existing skills to the degree possible—for example, some of the programs taught the refugee women to operate power sewing machines.

Craft cooperatives have been another way to help refugee women augment their family income. Cottage Crafts, a language training and cottage industry/employment program, served mainly Hmong women. The women received initial counseling in their own homes and volunteer tutors taught English. Because of the project, the Hmong established a cooperative Asian food and gift store. It also generated increased income for participants who obtained full- or part-time jobs.

CONCLUSION

Admission to an industrialized country presents many challenges for refugee women. Whether they enter as asylum seekers or through a resettlement program, whether they come from a developing country or an industrialized one, issues of adjustment and integration must be resolved. Effective programs have been established in a number of settings, programs that can be used as models to improve efforts to help refugee women adapt to their new surroundings. Most importantly, governments and nongovernmental organizations should facilitate the empowerment of resettled women through support for self-help groups, provision of information about the rights of refugee women, and increased collaboration between refugee women and women already resident in the country.

NOTES

Full citations can be found in the select bibliography.

1. Tenhula, *Voices from Southeast Asia*, 122–23.
2. UNHCR, *Resettlement Handbook*, revised edition, July 2002.
3. UNHCR, *Resettlement Handbook*, iv, 12.
4. UNHCR, *Resettlement Handbook*.
5. UNHCR, *Resettlement Handbook*, iv, 13.
6. Under the Immigration and Refugee Protection Act of 2002, Canada has shifted more generally toward protection rather than ability to establish as criteria for resettlement.
7. Noreen Spencer-Simmons, "Refugee Women at Risk: A Canadian Case Study," Paper prepared for a meeting of the UN Division for the Advancement of Women Doc. No. EGM/RDWC/1990/CS.4-2 (July 1990).
8. Appendix to UNHCR, *Resettlement Handbook*, prepared by Canadian government (2002).
9. June Chua, "Becoming Canadian." Available at www.cbc.ca/news/becoming-canadian/govtsponsored.html (2002).
10. Irmtraud Weissinger, "Cultural Adjustment: Experiences in Work with Eritrean Women," in *Working with Refugee Women*, ed. N. Kelly, 157.
11. Refugee Policy Group, *New Branches . . . Distant Roots*, summary of a symposium on older refugees in the United States, June 1988 (Washington, D.C.: Refugee Policy Group, 1988).

12. *Working with Refugee Women*, ed. N. Kelly, 59.

13. Lewin/ICF and Refugee Policy Group, *Promoting Mental Health Services*.

14. Nathan Caplan, John K. Whitmore, and Quang L. Bui, *Southeast Asian Refugee Self-Sufficiency Study: Final Report* (Ann Arbor, Mich.: Institute for Social Research, 1985).

15. Northwest Regional Educational Laboratory, *A Study of English Language Training for Refugees in the United States, Vols. 1–3* (Portland, Ore.: Northwest Regional Educational Laboratory, 1982–1984).

16. Northwest Regional Educational Laboratory, *A Study of English Language Training*.

17. World University Service, "The Education of Refugee Women, with Special Reference to the Case of Great Britain," reprinted in *Working with Refugee Women*.

18. WUS, "The Education of Refugee Women in Britain: A Case Study in Resettlement," reprinted in *Working with Refugee Women*.

19. Eileen Pittaway, "We Want Help, Not Charity: Refugee Women in Australia Speak about Their Own Resettlement Needs," prepared for a meeting of the UN Division for the Advancement of Women, Doc. No. EGM/RDWC/1990/CS.1-2, July 1990.

20. Inger Boesen and Kim Pedersen, *Refugee Women in Denmark: Towards a New Identity?* (Copenhagen: Danish Refugee Council, 1988), 5.

21. Nathan Caplan, et al., *Southeast Asian Refugee Self-Sufficiency Study*.

22. Susan Forbes (Martin), *Adaptation and Integration of Recent Refugees in the United States* (Washington, D.C.: Refugee Policy Group, 1985), 6.

23. Suzanne Stiver Lie, "Immigrant Women and Their Work: A Study of British, Yugoslavian and Chilean Immigrant Women in Norway," *Scandinavian Journal of Development Alternatives* 2, no. 3 (1983): 65.

24. U.S. Office of Refugee Resettlement, *Annual Report to Congress*, 2001.

25. U.S. Office of Refugee Resettlement, *Annual Report to Congress*.

26. Lie, "Immigrant Women and their Work."

27. Quoted in Elzbieta Gozdziak, *Older Refugees in the United States: From Dignity to Despair* (Washington, D.C.: Refugee Policy Group, 1988), 26.

28. Abby Spero, *In America and In Need: Immigrant, Refugee and Entrant Women* (Washington, D.C.: American Association of Community and Junior Colleges and the U.S. Department of Labor Women's Bureau, 1985), 137.

29. Gozdziak, "Older Refugees," 38.

30. Quoted in Helena Moussa, "Women Refugees: Cultural Adjustment as Empowerment," in *Working with Refugee Women*, 152

31. Refugee Women in Development, *The Quilting Bee* (Potomac, Md. and Washington, D.C.: Texpress Publishing Group, 1988).

32. Working Group on Refugee Women, Paris, "Refugee Women and Cultural Adjustment: A Case Study," printed in *Working with Refugee Women*, 154.

33. Spero, *In America and In Need*, 139.

Refugee Women in Kenya. (Susan Martin)

8

Responses to the Situation of Refugee Women

The General Assembly, noting with great concern that women and children constitute the majority of refugees and displaced persons in most areas . . . urges the international community to provide urgent and adequate assistance to all refugee and displaced women and to developing countries providing asylum or rehabilitation, especially the least developed and most seriously affected countries.[1]

Following years of inattention to the needs and resources of refugee and displaced women, a new awareness and willingness to take gender into account in policy development and implementation has emerged. This chapter reviews efforts to improve responses to refugee women in the UN system as well as by nongovernmental organizations (NGOs).

UN INITIATIVES ON REFUGEE WOMEN

In December 1975, the General Assembly proclaimed 1976–1985 as the UN Decade for Women: Equality, Development, and Peace. A World Plan of Action was adopted. By the end of five years, when a mid-decade review would be held, some minimum goals were to be met in terms of increased literacy, equal access to education, increased employment, equal eligibility for the vote, greater participation of women in policy-making positions, increased provision of health services, and recognition of the economic value of women's work at home. Special attention was drawn to the situation of migrant women in the World Plan of Action, recognizing that they faced special problems.

The mid-decade meeting took place in Copenhagen in July 1980. Specific resolutions relating to refugee and displaced women were adopted by that conference. In addition to some general recommendations about the causes of refugee movements and the responsibilities of states to protect and assist refugees, the report included the following recommendations regarding refugee women:

- it strongly urged governments to bring to justice those who abuse refugee women and children and to take steps to prevent such abuses;
- it urged UNHCR, in cooperation with other concerned UN agencies, to establish programs necessary for dealing with the special needs of displaced and refugee women, especially in the areas of health, education, and employment;
- it urged UNHCR to develop and implement programs of resettlement and family reunification, including special programs for reuniting unaccompanied children with their families;
- it recommended that UNHCR increase the number of women at all levels of its staff and establish a high-level position or coordinator of women's programs; and
- it requested that family planning information and methods should be available on a voluntary and nationally acceptable basis to both refugee men and women.

More specifically, the Program of Action for the second half of the decade called for assistance and counseling to women refugees, with an emphasis on the development of self-reliance; special health care measures and health counseling by women medical workers where necessary; supplemental feeding programs for pregnant and lactating women; training and educational programs including orientation, language, and job training; income generation programs; and sufficient international personnel in refugee camps to discourage exploitation and attacks on refugee women.

Little progress was made in implementing these recommendations during the next five years. Some efforts were made, however, to gain greater understanding of the needs of refugee women. For example, in 1981 the Intergovernmental Committee for Migration held a seminar on the adaptation and integration of refugee and migrant women.

The meeting in Nairobi marking the end of the decade on women served as an impetus for further action in 1985. UNHCR organized a Roundtable on Refugee Women in April 1985. The Roundtable included a number of prominent women, including cabinet ministers, ambassadors, and others who would be involved in the Nairobi meeting. Also, a number of governmental delegations made the issue a priority for discussion at Nairobi. The U.S. government, for example, provided funds for a study of refugee women that was to develop recommendations its delegation could bring to the conference. Nongovernmental organizations came with specific recommendations for improvements as well.

In the years after Nairobi and the inclusion of specific reference to refugee women in the Forward Looking Strategies (paragraphs 298 and 299), interest in the issue of refugee women grew further among donor governments and within UNHCR. In October 1985, the Executive Committee of the UNHCR, for the first time, included the issue of refugee women on its agenda and adopted a conclusion on the protection of refugee women. In 1987, the Executive Committee of the UNHCR called upon the High Commissioner to report in detail at its next session on the particular protection and assistance problems and needs of refugee women and on the concrete measures taken to meet them. In February 1988, UNHCR established a Steering Committee on Refugee Women, under the chairmanship of the deputy high commissioner, to define, oversee, and coordinate a process of assessing, strengthening, and reorienting existing policies and programs. Then, in August 1988, internal guidelines on the international protection of refugee women were issued to all substantive officers in the field and at headquarters.

A Note on Refugee Women was prepared for the meeting of the Executive Committee in 1988. The note summarized the various protection and assistance issues facing refugee women and described the current and planned action of UNHCR. Field offices were requested to provide more detailed information and follow-up on protection problems affecting refugee women. The data systems for collecting information on refugees were reviewed with an aim toward increasing their capacity to capture gender-specific information. Efforts also began to identify institutional changes needed to ensure that the needs of refugee women were systematically considered and addressed; to raise the level of visibility given to refugee women's issues; and to develop training materials to sensitize UNHCR, host country government, and NGO staff.

A new position was created to ensure that these activities were productive: a senior coordinator for refugee women. Canada provided a major impetus for this appointment and seconded a senior staff member to fill the position. Her duties included: coordinating and monitoring the process of integrating women's issues throughout the organization; preparing a policy framework to include refugee women in all levels of program and project planning and implementation; reviewing existing programs and procedures to ensure full participation of refugee women; identifying appropriate action-oriented research on specific women's issues; contributing to the

review and assessment of protection and assistance programs; and assist
ing in the development of training programs on gender impact analysis.
The office subsequently was renamed the Office of Senior Coordinator
for Refugee Women and Gender Equality, as a way to emphasize the need
to mainstream women and gender issues into the totality of UNHCR's
work.

The report submitted to the Executive Committee in 1989 described continued problems for refugee women (particularly regarding physical protection) but it detailed progress at UNHCR in addressing the concerns:

- an evaluation of the protection guidelines found them to be of value and
  showed revisions needed to improve them;
- instructions had gone out to field offices that they must ensure that proposed program plans addressed the special needs of refugee women and
  children and took into account the ways in which they could contribute
  to the success of refugee programs;
- means of verifying the level of integration of women's concerns into programming was developed;
- an analytical framework for assessing the situation of refugee women
  was developed;
- the terms of reference for all field missions conducted by the Technical
  Support Unit included needs assessment of the situation of refugee
  women;
- the need for a primary health care approach with emphasis on women
  and children was reaffirmed and recommendations were made that at
  least 50 percent of the health workers be women;
- the special emergency needs of refugee women received increased attention in the UNHCR *Handbook for Emergencies*; and
- the needs of refugee women were to be taken into account in all refugee
  aid and development programs and projects.

Recognizing the need for more information on refugee women, the Office
embarked on several research projects on specific countries and issues, such
as education. The Technical Support Service also engaged in several field
missions aimed at assessing the situation of refugee women in specific locations, such as Guinea, Côte d'Ivoire, and Hong Kong.

Recognizing the importance of trained and sensitive staff, UNHCR intro-
duced a course in gender impact analysis for refugee assistance projects. The
course was designed to ensure that project planners and implementers perform a thorough analysis of the situation of women in any refugee population,
based on an examination of the gender-based division of socioeconomic

roles. Referred to as People-Oriented Planning, the training uses a case study approach to demonstrate the importance of taking gender, age, and other characteristics into account in designing and implementing programs for refugees. Although recognized as beneficial training, because of high turnover and limited resources, too few UNHCR staff are exposed to the concepts behind People-Oriented Planning.

In 1989, the UNHCR Executive Committee requested the High Commissioner to provide a policy framework and organizational work plan to be submitted at its next session. The major thrust of the policy statement approved by the Executive Committee in 1990 is the integration of considerations regarding the special needs and resources of refugee women into all aspects of UNHCR's protection and assistance activities. Referred to as mainstreaming, the policy sought to ensure recognition that becoming a refugee affects men and women differently and that effective programming must recognize these differences. The policy further recognized that refugee women must themselves participate in the planning and implementation of projects. Refugee women, under this framework, are to be thought of not just as vulnerable people requiring assistance but also as resources for their own and their communities' development.[2]

The Thirty-fourth Session of the Commission on the Status of Women provided a forum for heightening awareness of the situation of refugee women, particularly in the broader range of UN agencies. To prepare for the meeting, the Division for the Advancement of Women held an experts' meeting that outlined specific recommendations to improve the responsiveness of the UN system to the needs of refugee women. The meeting involved UNHCR, UNRWA, UNICEF, various NGOs, and other relevant organizations.

The Expert Group emphasized the importance of ensuring that the civil, political, social, and cultural rights of refugee and displaced women and children are reaffirmed and backed by laws, policies, and programs. Governments, relevant UN agencies, and concerned nongovernmental organizations were called upon to redouble their efforts to respond to the specific needs of refugee and displaced women and children, including by addressing the root causes of these situations in an urgent manner.

The Expert Group further recommended that gender-sensitive staff, women in particular, be recruited and advanced to management and field positions in international organizations, national governments, and nongovernmental organizations in order to provide appropriate assistance and protection to refugee and displaced women. Key staff of organizations working with refugees and displaced persons should receive training to help them respond more effectively to the presence and needs of refugee and displaced women. This finding followed closely the recommendations of the 1990 Permanent

Working Group on the Situation of Women in UNHCR report on inadequacies in staffing:

> The status of women in UNHCR remains extremely feeble. Though [the proportion of women is] high among the G[eneral] S[upport] staff, the proportions are considerably lower than those of males in the [professional] categories. The presence of women in the most senior grades, in particular, leaves much to be desired.[3]

The Working Group recommended increasing the proportion of women professional staff at both the central and field levels in the interest of equity as well as effective performance. Noting that the majority of refugees are women and children, the Working Group referenced the important role that women staff at UNHCR could play in ensuring greater participation of refugee women.

The Expert Group called upon the international agencies to increase their capacity to respond to the needs of refugee and displaced women and children and to coordinate more effectively their efforts. The UN and other international and regional organizations, governments, nongovernmental organizations, and funding agencies which play a role in the protection of and/or assistance to refugees and displaced persons were encouraged to adopt their own policy statements on refugee and displaced women and children, including a time frame for implementation.

In 1991, the UNHCR issued *Guidelines on the Protection of Refugee Women*, which outlined concrete steps that could be taken to increase international protection for refugee and displaced women. With regard to legal protection, the *Guidelines* recommended improvements in refugee determination standards and procedures to increase the access of women and children. The *Guidelines* also urged implementation of measures to ensure greater protection from physical violence, sexual abuse, abduction, and those circumstances which force women and children into prostitution and other illegal activities. In 1995, UNHCR issued further guidance to promote the protection of refugee women in *Sexual Violence against Refugees: Guidelines on Prevention and Response*.

Recognizing the close link between protection and assistance measures in addressing the needs of refugee women, the *Guidelines* recommended that protection concerns be borne in mind when planning and implementing assistance programs. They also included detailed recommendations to improve both emergency and longer-term assistance to refugee and displaced women and children, emphasizing that greater attention should be given to combating malnutrition, improving the health condition of refugee and displaced women and children, increasing access to safe drinking water, constructing adequate and appropriate shelter, and providing the mechanisms for increased self-reliance through education programs, employment, and income generation.

Further, the *Guidelines* emphasized that assistance and protection activities could only be truly effective if refugee and displaced women themselves are full partners in the process of assessing their needs, planning and implementing programs, and all other decisions that affect their lives. The full participation of refugee and displaced women in assistance and protection activities was also seen as an integral part of efforts to find longer-term solutions to refugee situations.

The *Guidelines on the Protection of Refugee Women, Sexual Violence against Refugees: Guidelines on Prevention and Response*, and other materials on refugee women have been widely disseminated within the agency and to its implementing partners. They were also incorporated into training programs for staff working in refugee crises as well as handbooks and operating instructions for the various assistance programs discussed in the *Guidelines*. In the context of the Global Consultations on International Protection, which marked the fiftieth anniversary of the UN Convention Relating to the Status of Refugees, UNHCR has also issued new guidance on assessing gender-based claims to refugee status. Programming to support reproductive health services, gender-based violence counseling, and the various postconflict women's initiatives discussed in earlier chapters also reflect growing interest during the 1990s in meeting the needs of refugee women.

Assessments of the effectiveness of efforts to respond to the needs and opportunities presented by refugee women generally find there has been an increased level of awareness within humanitarian agencies of the needs of refugee women, but, as the most recent evaluation of implementation of the *Guidelines on Protection of Refugee Women* stated, "Overall, implementation of the *Guidelines* was found to be uneven and incomplete, occurring on an ad hoc basis in certain sites rather than in a globally consistent and systematic way. Positive actions tend to be sporadic, and they are often insufficient to provide refugee women with equitable protection."[4] Improvements in assisting and protecting refugee women have been impeded by overall financial cuts in refugee budgets, combined with inadequacies in staffing that lead to inadequate field presence of protection personnel.

Progress within the United Nations on protection of internally displaced women is even more halting, largely because there is little agreement on responsibility for internally displaced persons (IDPs) protection in general. The *Guiding Principles on Internal Displacement* makes clear the need to take gender into account in ensuring protection from, during, and following internal displacement. Throughout the *Guiding Principles* are specific guidance on the participation of women and children in decisions on displacement as well as the need to ensure that women and children have access to assistance as well as legal protection and physical safety and security.

Even though progress has been made in setting out protection standards through the *Guiding Principles*, violations of these guidelines are rampant. National governments retain the principal responsibility for protecting their citizens, but they may have neither the will nor the capacity to carry out these obligations. In many situations, governments are outwardly hostile to the internally displaced persons within their territory. Unlike in refugee situations, where UNHCR's mandate is clear, there is no comparable institutional locus of responsibility for international protection of IDPs when sovereign states are unwilling or unable to fulfill their responsibilities.

Recognizing that effective humanitarian aid and protection of internally displaced persons is still inadequate, the UN Office for the Coordination of Humanitarian Affairs (OCHA) formed a unit specifically responsible for IDPs that began work in January 2002. Small, nonoperational, and composed of staff largely drawn from other UN agencies, the unit's terms of reference set out the following activities: promotion and support of advocacy efforts; monitoring of situations of internal displacement in order to identify operational gaps in the responses to internal displacement; provision of training, guidance, and expertise to Resident and Humanitarian Coordinators, UN Country Teams, and humanitarian organizations on IDP-related issues, and the formulation of strategies to address the protection, humanitarian, and durable development needs of IDPs; development of necessary linkages between the humanitarian response to internal displacement and the security, political, and development spheres of activity; mobilization of the resources needed to assist IDPs; and further development of interagency policies on IDP issues. In cooperation with the secretary general's representative on IDPs, the unit is assigned responsibility for bringing greater attention to the *Guiding Principles on Internal Displacement* and encouraging additional governments to comply with these emerging international standards.

To carry out its mandate, the office requires sustained and adequate funding, capable staff, the commitment of the secretary general to support the unit's efforts on behalf of IDPs, as well as the financial and political support of the principal donors. Even with such support, as a small office within a larger bureaucratic structure, the unit faces serious challenges to its ability to carry out the activities spelled out in the terms of references. While the unit may develop effective strategies to protect, assist, and find durable solutions for IDPs, it is reliant on the willingness of other UN agencies to take on the operational responsibility to implement the strategy. Persuasion remains the principal tool available to the unit to improve responses, but with tight budgets and difficult issues of sovereignty and security to overcome, persuasion without authority over budgets and operations may not be sufficient to fill gaps in UN response, particularly regarding protection of the rights of internally displaced women and children.

When he was U.S. Ambassador to the United Nations, Richard Holbrooke recommended that full responsibility for IDPs be assigned to UNHCR. He pointed out that IDPs were, in fact, internal refugees. Given UNHCR's extensive experience assisting and protecting international refugees, it would have the greatest capacity for undertaking similar efforts on behalf of those who were internally displaced. But a number of hurdles remain. In addition to concerns about the adequacy of resources, UNHCR fears that countries of asylum will refuse admission to refugees if they believe that UNHCR is protecting the internally displaced, further eroding what UNHCR sees as its primary mandate—to maintain first asylum and protect refugees from *refoulement* (forced return) to situations in which they may be endangered.[5]

The International Committee of the Red Cross (ICRC) would be another possibility for taking on explicit responsibility for protection of IDPs, building on its responsibilities under the Geneva Conventions for civilians in armed conflict situations. As with UNHCR, ICRC has the experience and expertise to undertake protection activities on behalf of IDPs, many already coming under its mandate. ICRC's role is quite limited, however, when internal displacement comes from causes other than armed conflict. IDPs forced to leave their homes because of repression, political instability, generalized violence, environmental degradation, natural disasters, and development projects would not come within ICRC's existing mandate, but these displaced persons may be equally in need of protection if their own governments are unwilling or unable to assist and protect them. An expansion of ICRC's protection activities to include at least those displaced by generalized violence and ethnic tension would seem consistent, however, with their mandate.

A further possibility would be the UN High Commissioner for Human Rights (UNHCHR). UNHCHR has broad responsibility for preventing and protecting victims of human rights abuses. The agency already provides support to the secretary general's representative on internally displaced persons, who routinely investigates and reports on protection problems facing IDPs and who developed and presented the *Guiding Principles on Internal Displacement*. It has had a weak field presence, however, and has not generally taken on operational responsibilities.

The secretary general, on the recommendation of OCHA's IDP unit, could assign responsibility on a case-by-case basis, judging which agency has the

field presence and capacity in specific countries. This process would be flexible, but the agency requested to undertake protection in a particular situation
would not necessarily have the resources or will to accept the responsibility.
A more formal and permanent process would give one of the agencies listed
above the explicit mandate for protection of IDPs. Going further, responsibility for all assistance and protection of forced migrants—refugees and IDPs
alike—could be consolidated into a single organization—perhaps a UN High
Commissioner for Forced Migration.

NONGOVERNMENTAL ORGANIZATIONS

The NGO community's involvement in issues pertaining to refugee women
has closely paralleled that of the UN system. NGOs have been pivotal
forces in lobbying governments and the UN system to take needed actions
to improve responses to the situation of refugee women. The NGOs have
also looked at their own roles in implementing policies that will allow for
more effective programs for refugee women. Prior to the Nairobi conference, NGOs in a number of countries wrote and held meetings about the situation of refugee women and promoted greater attention to their situation.
Organizations concerned about refugees participated in the NGO meetings
surrounding the Nairobi conference. Workshops focused specifically on this
issue.

The principal locus internationally of NGO involvement during the late
1980s and early 1990s was the NGO Working Group on Refugee Women. A
coalition of interested individuals from about 100 NGOs throughout the
world, the Working Group kept its members informed of developments and
convened meetings to coincide with the Executive Committee meetings at
UNHCR.

An international consultation organized by the Working Group was held
in November 1988. The consultation brought together about 150 representatives from refugee women's groups, NGOs, intergovernmental organizations, and governments to consider how refugee women's issues can be
more effectively addressed by the international community. The meeting
was organized around five major themes: protection, health, education, employment, and cultural adjustment. The participants developed specific recommendations pertaining to these areas. Following the consultation, a report was prepared entitled *Working with Refugee Women: A Practical
Guide*. The guide includes analyses of the five themes, specific recommendations for action, background papers, and personal stories by and about
refugee women.

Groups have also developed in individual countries, some examining the policies within their own countries and others focusing on international assistance and protection. For example, the Women's Commission for Refugee Women and Children was established in the United States to speak in support of improved policies and programs for refugee and displaced women. An Australian National Consultative Committee on Refugee Women also was formed with the aim of improving the quality of life of refugee women, networking both internationally and nationally and being the focal point for the expression of the concerns of refugee women.

CHALLENGES AHEAD

The development of policies and guidelines related to the protection of and assistance to refugee women and children has provided a useful framework for increasing the capacity of the international system to respond to the needs of these populations. The test of the success of these policies and guidelines are in their implementation. As discussed above, knowledge and even agreement with the *Guidelines on the Protection of Refugee Women* has not always translated into concrete actions to improve protection. In fact, the recommendations offered in the first edition of this book to close the gap between rhetoric and reality remain as needed today as a decade ago:

- mechanisms must be developed to actually integrate refugee women's and children's issues into all stages of program planning, implementation, monitoring, and evaluation;
- country-specific and sector-specific policies and procedures must be reviewed and revised, as necessary, to reflect the policies on refugee women and children;
- needs assessments and data collection must provide a more accurate representation of the refugee population; and
- more effective and creative programs must be implemented if the needs of refugee women and children are to be met.

The special needs and resources of refugee women are now well documented. The challenge for the future is to translate our improved understanding of their situation into concrete, effective programs which will help them live in safety and dignity. If any lesson is to be learned from the past, it is the importance of including refugee women in all aspects of program design and implementation. They are the best judges of their needs and aspirations.

NOTES

Full citations can be found in the select bibliography.

1. UN General Assembly, *Refugee and Displaced Women,* Resolution 35/135, (New York: United Nations, 1980).
2. UNHCR, *Policy on Refugee Women* (Geneva: UNHCR, 1990).
3. Permanent Working Group on the Situation of Women in UNHCR, Report, Geneva, 1990, 2.
4. Women's Commission, *UNHCR Policy*, 2.
5. Ironically, UNHCR's own programs to assist refugees repatriate to their home countries often lead to massive increases in internal displacement, as returning refugees find they cannot go back to their home villages (generally because of continued instability, landmines, or lack of economic opportunities) and have to relocate to other parts of the country.

Select Bibliography

African Training and Research Centre for Women. *Refugee and Displaced Women in Independent African States*. Addis Ababa: Economic Commission for Africa, 1986.

Ager, Alastair. "Mental Health Issues in Refugee Populations: A Review." Working Paper of the Harvard Center for the Study of Culture and Medicine (July 1993).

Agger, Inger. "Sexual Torture of Political Prisoners: An Overview." *Journal of Traumatic Stress* 2, no. 3 (1989).

Ahmed 1993 FCJ 718 Canada FCA 1993.

Aitchison, Roberta. "Reluctant Witnesses." *Cultural Survival Quarterly* 8, no. 2 (Summer 1984).

American College of Obstetricians and Gynecologists. "Female Circumcision/Female Genital Mutilation (FC/FGM) Fact Sheet." Available at www.acog.org/from_home/departments/dept_notice.cfm?recno=18&bulletin=1081 (n.d.).

Amnesty International. *Women in the Front Line: Human Rights Violations against Women*. New York: Amnesty International Publications, 1991.

———. "Medical Letter Writing Action, Conditions in 'Regroupment' Camps, Burundi." AI Index: AFR 16/036/99 (1999).

———. "Nigeria: Condemnation of the Death Penalty. Concerns on the Implementation of New Sharia-Based Penal Codes." Available at www.amnesty.org.au/women/action-letter09.html (March 26, 2003).

Anderson, Mary B. and Peter J. Woodrow. *Rising from the Ashes: Development Strategies in Times of Disaster*. Boulder, Colo.: Westview Press, 1989.

BBC News. "Pakistan Court Rules on Adultery." Available at news.bbc.co.uk/2/low/south_asia/22208171.stm (August 21, 2002).

Billard, Annick. "Women and Health in Afghan Refugee Camps." *Refugees* 2 (1983).

Boesen, Inger and Kim Pedersen. *Refugee Women in Denmark: Towards a New Identity?* Copenhagen: Danish Refugee Council, 1988.

Caplan, Nathan, John K. Whitmore, and Quang L. Bui. *Southeast Asian Refugee Self-Sufficiency Study: Final Report*. Ann Arbor, Mich.: Institute for Social Research, 1985.

Chambers, Robert. *Rural Refugees in Africa: Past Experience, Future Pointers*. New York: Ford Foundation, 1984.

——. "Hidden Losers? The Impact of Rural Refugees and Refugee Programs on Poorer Hosts." *International Migration Review* 20, no. 2 (1986).

Chua, June. "Becoming Canadian." Available at www.cbc.ca/news/becomingcanadian/govtsponsored.html (2002).

Clark, Lance. *Refugee Participation Case Study: The Shaba Settlements in Zaire*. Washington, D.C.: Refugee Policy Group, 1987.

——. *Refugee Participation: Changing Talk into Action*. Washington, D.C.: Refugee Policy Group, 1987.

Coffey, Margaret. "Visiting Women on the West Bank." Available at www.austcare.org.au/content/west_bank_women.htm (n.d.).

Cohen, Roberta. *Human Rights at the UN: Internally Displaced People Need Human Rights Protection*. New York: International League for Human Rights, 1990.

——. *Refugee and Internally Displaced Women: A Development Perspective*. The Brookings Institute—Refugee Policy Group Project on Internal Displacement, November 1995.

——. "Protecting Internally Displaced Women and Children." In Wendy Davies, ed. *Rights Have No Borders: Worldwide Internal Displacement*. Norwegian Refugee Council/Global IDP Survey, 1998.

Connor, Kerry M. *Skill Inventory of Afghan Women Refugees in the North West Frontier and Baluchistan Provinces*. Islamabad: UNICEF, 1988.

Corren, Chris. *Gender Audit of Reconstruction Programmes in South Eastern Europe*. (Urgent Action Fund and Women's Commission for Refugee Women and Children, June 2000).

Crisp, Jeff. "No Solutions in Sight: The Problem of Protracted Refugee Situations in Africa." UNHCR Working Paper No. 75 (January 2003).

Cuny, Fred C. *Refugee Participation in Emergency Relief Operations*. Washington, D.C.: Refugee Policy Group, 1987.

Demirkaya v SSHD (CA) [1999] INLR 441, [1999] Imm AR 498.

Deng, Francis. *Report of the Representative of the Secretary General on IDPs, Commission on Human Rights, E/CN.4/1995/50*. United Nations, February 2, 1995.

——. *Report of the Representative of the Secretary-General on IDPs, Commission on Human Rights, E/CN.4/1996/52*. United Nations, February 22, 1996, paragraphs 45–56.

——. "Forced Relocation in Burundi, Report of the Representative of the Secretary General on Internally Displaced Persons." Doc. E/CN.4/2001/5/Add.1. Available at http://193.194.138.190/Huridocda/Huridoca.nsf/TestFrame/aff2c994e03ca244c12569d000471a5d?Opendocument (March 2000).

Dunkley, Glen. *Review of UNHCR's Refugee Education Activities*. Geneva: UNHCR, 1997.

Dupree, Nancy Hatch. "The Role of Afghan Women after Repatriation." *Writer's Union for a Free Afghanistan*, Peshawar (1988).

Dutch Ministry of Social Affairs and Labour. *Sexual Violence against Women Refugees*. The Hague: Dutch Ministry of Social Affairs and Labour, 1984.

El-Bushra, Judy, Asha El-Karib, and Angela Hadjipateras. "Gender-Sensitive Programme Design and Planning in Conflict-Affected Situations." ACORD, ESCOR Project R 7501. Available at www.acord.org.uk/Publications/G&CResearch/ (January 2002).

Fatin v INS 12F. 3d 1233 (3rd Cir. 1993).

Ferris, Elizabeth. *Refugee Women and Violence*. Geneva: World Council of Churches, 1990.

Forbes (Martin), Susan. *Adaptation and Integration of Recent Refugees in the United States*. Washington, D.C.: Refugee Policy Group, 1985.

Giacaman, Rita. "Palestinian Women in the Uprising: From Followers to Leaders." *Journal of Refugee Studies* 2, no. 1 (1989).

Goodwin-Gill, Guy. *The Refugee in International Law*. Oxford: Oxford University Press, 1996.

Gozdziak, Elzbieta. *Older Refugees in the United States: From Dignity to Despair*. Washington, D.C.: Refugee Policy Group, April 1988.

Hall, Eve. "Vocational Training for Women Refugees in Africa: Guidelines from Selected Field Projects, Training Policies Discussion Paper No. 26." (Geneva: International Labour Organization, 1988).

Holtzman, Steven. "Rethinking 'Relief' and 'Development' in Transitions from Conflict." Prepared for the Brookings Initiative on Relief and Development (January 1999).

Human Rights Watch. "Human Rights Watch Applauds Rwanda Rape Verdict: Sets International Precedent for Punishing Sexual Violence as a War Crime." Available at www.hrw.org/press98/sept/rrape902.htm (September 2, 1998).

———. *Emptying the Hills, Regroupment in Burundi*. Available at www.hrw.org/reports/2000/burundi2/ (June 2000).

Immigration and Refugee Board. "Women Refugee Claimants Fearing Gender-Related Persecution." (November 13, 1996).

Islam v SSHD; R v IAT ex parte Shah (HL) [1999] INLR 144, [1999] Imm AR 283.

Jaranson, James, Susan Forbes Martin, and Solvig Ekblad. "Refugee Mental Health: Issues for the New Millennium." In *Mental Health United States: 2000*. Available at www.mentalhealth.org/publications/allpubs/SMA01-3537/chapter13.asp (2000).

Kabeer, Naila. *The Conditions and Consequences of Choice: Reflections on the Measure of Empowerment*. Geneva: UNRISD, 1999.

Kelly, Ninette, ed. *Working with Refugee Women: A Practical Guide*. Geneva: International NGO Working Group on Refugee Women, 1989.

Krill, Francoise. *The Protection of Women in International Humanitarian Law*. Geneva: International Committee of the Red Cross, 1985.

Krummel, Sharon. *Refugee Women and the Experience of Cultural Uprooting*. Geneva: Refugee Service, World Council of Churches, n.d.

Kumar, Krishna, ed. *Women and Women's Organizations in Post-Conflict Societies: The Role of International Assistance*. Washington, D.C. and Boulder, Colo.: Lynne Reinner, 2000.

Lewin/ICF and Refugee Policy Group. *Promoting Mental Health Services for Refugees: A Handbook on Model Practices*. Washington, D.C.: Office of Refugee Resettlement, 1990.

Lie, Suzanne Stiver. "Immigrant Women and Their Work: A Study of British, Yugoslavian and Chilean Immigrant Women in Norway." *Scandinavian Journal of Development Alternatives* 2, no. 3 (1983).

Lynch, James, F. *Border Khmer: A Democratic Study of the Residents of Site 2, Site B, and Site 8.* Bangkok: Ford Foundation, 1989.

Mahalingam, Suba. "Education: Protecting the Rights of Displaced Children." *Forced Migration Review* 15 (October 2002).

Manz, Beatrice. *Refugees of a Hidden War: The Aftermath of Counterinsurgency in Guatemala.* Albany: State University of New York Press, 1987.

———. *Repatriation and Reintegration: An Arduous Process in Guatemala.* Washington, D.C.: Hemispheric Migration Project, Center for Immigration Policy and Refugee Assistance, Georgetown University, 1988.

Martin, Susan Forbes. *Handbook for Implementing the Guiding Principles on Internal Displacement.* New York: UN Office for the Coordination of Humanitarian Affairs, 1999.

Martin, Susan Forbes and Emily Copeland. *Making Ends Meet? Refugee Women and Income Generation.* Washington, D.C.: Refugee Policy Group, 1987.

Mertus, Julie A., Jasmina Tesanovic, Habiba Metikos, and Rada Boric, eds. *The Suitcase: Refugee Voices from Bosnia and Croatia.* Berkeley: University of California Press, 1997.

Mertus, Julie A. W*ar's Offensive on Women: The Humanitarian Challenge in Bosnia, Kosovo, and Afghanistan.* Bloomfield, Conn.: Kumarian Press, 2000.

Miserez, Diana, ed. *Refugees: The Trauma of Exile.* Dordrecht: Martinus Nijhoff, 1988.

Northwest Regional Educational Laboratory. *A Study of English Language Training for Refugees in the United States, Vols. 1–3.* Portland, Ore.: Northwest Regional Educational Laboratory, 1982–1984.

Overhagen, Mei Ying Van. "Refugee Women and International Relief Programs," in *Refugees in the World: The European Community's Response.* Utrecht: Sim Special Issue 10, 1990.

Pittaway, Eileen. "We Want Help, Not Charity: Refugee Women in Australia Speak about Their Own Resettlement Needs." Prepared for meeting of the UN Division for the Advancement of Women Doc. No. EGM/RDWC/1990/CS.1-2 (July 1990).

Purdin, Susan J. "Lessons from West Africa." *Sexual Health Exchange,* no. 2. Available at www.kit.nl/information_services/exchange_content/html/2000_2_lessons_from_west_afric.asp (2000).

"Refugee Aid and Development." Executive Committee, Thirty-fourth Session (AIAC 96/627) report of the meeting of experts (September 12, 1983).

Refugee Policy Group. *New Branches . . . Distant Roots.* Washington, D.C.: Refugee Policy Group, 1988.

Refugee Women in Development. *The Quilting Bee.* Potomac, Md. and Washington, D.C.: Texpress Publishing Group, 1988.

Refugees International. "Burundian Regroupment Camps: A Man-Made Humanitarian Emergency, an Impediment to Peace." (January 20, 2000).

———. "Conditions in Burundian Camps Rapidly Deteriorating." (March 1, 2000).

Reproductive Health Outlook. "Refugee Reproductive Health, Program Examples." Available at www.rho.org/html/refugee_progexamples.htm#topofpage (n.d.).

Reynell, Josephine. *Political Pawns*. Oxford: Refugee Studies Programme, 1989.

Rome Statute. A/CONF.183/9 of July 17, 1998 and corrected by procès-verbaux of November 10, 1998; July 12, 1999; November 30, 1999; May 8, 2000; January 17, 2001; and January 16, 2002.

Roulet-Billard, Annick. "First Person Feminine." *Refugees* 70 (1989).

Spencer-Simmons, Noreen. "Refugee Women at Risk: A Canadian Case Study." Paper prepared for a meeting of the UN Division for the Advancement of Women DOC. No. EGM/RDWC/1990/CS.4-2 (July 1990).

Sphere Project. *Humanitarian Charter and Minimum Standards in Disaster Response*. Geneva: Sphere Project, 1998.

Spiegel, Paul, M. Sheik, P. Salama, and C. Crawford. "Health Programs and Policies Associated with Decreased Mortality in Displaced People in Post-Emergency Phase Camps: A Retrospective Study." *Lancet* (December 12, 2002).

Snyder, Margaret. *Women: The Key to Ending Hunger*. New York: The Hunger Project, 1990.

Spero, Abby. *In America and in Need: Immigrant, Refugee and Entrant Women*. Washington, D.C.: American Association of Community and Junior Colleges and the U.S. Department of Labor Women's Bureau, 1985.

Tenhula, John. *Voices from Southeast Asia: The Refugee Experience in the United States*. New York: Holmes and Meicr, 1991.

Thomas, Angharad and Gordon Wilson. "Technological Capabilities in Textile Production in Sahrawai Refugee Camps." *Journal of Refugee Studies* 9, no. 2 (1986).

U.K. Immigration Appellate Authority. "Asylum Gender Guidelines." Available at www.iaa.gov.uk/general_info/iaa_gender.htm (November 2000).

UN Commission on Human Rights. *Resolution on Internally Displaced Persons*. UNESC E/CN.4/1991/L.34. New York: United Nations, 1991.

UN Department of Economic and Social Affairs. *Popular Participation in Decision Making for Development*. New York: United Nations, 1975.

UN General Assembly. *Refugee and Displaced Women*. Resolution 35/135. New York: United Nations, 1980.

——. "Investigation into Sexual Exploitation of Refugees by Aid Workers in West Africa: Report of the Secretary-General on the Activities of the Office of Internal Oversight Services." A57/465 Fifty-seventh Session, Agenda item 122 (October 11, 2002).

UN High Commissioner for Refugees (UNHCR). *Handbook for Emergencies—Part One: Field Operations*. Geneva: UNHCR, 1982.

——. "Refugee Aid and Development." Executive Committee, Thirty-fourth Session (AIAC, 96/627) contains report of the meeting of experts (September 12, 1983).

——. *UNHCR and Refugee Women: International Protection*. Geneva: UNHCR, 1985.

——. "A Tale of Horror." *Refugees* 65 (1989).

——. *Refugee Women: A Selected and Annotated Bibliography* (revised and updated). Geneva: UNHCR Centre for Documentation on Refugees, 1989.

———. "A Dark Cloud." *Refugees* 72 (1990).

———. *Assessment of Global Resettlement Needs and Priorities for Refugees in 1991.* Geneva: UNHCR, 1990.

———. "Food Deficits and Nutritional Consequences in Ten Selected Refugee Populations." Prepared for a meeting with NGOs (1990).

———. *Note on Refugee Women and International Protection.* Geneva: UNHCR, 1990.

———. *Policy on Refugee Women.* Geneva: UNHCR, 1990.

———. *Report of the Permanent Working Group on the Situation of Women in UNHCR.* Geneva: UNHCR, 1990.

———. *A Framework for People-Oriented Planning in Refugee Situations.* Geneva: UNHCR, 1991.

———. *Guidelines on the Protection of Refugee Women.* Geneva: UNHCR, 1991.

———. *Handbook on Voluntary Repatriation: International Protection.* Geneva: UNHCR, 1996.

———. *Reproductive Health in Refugee Situations: An Inter-Agency Field Manual.* Geneva: UNHCR, 1999.

———. *Handbook for Emergencies.* Geneva: UNHCR, 2000.

———. *Statistical Yearbook.* Geneva: UNHCR, 2001.

———. Appendix to UNHCR, *Resettlement Handbook.* Prepared by the Canadian government (2002).

———. *Work with Young Refugees to Ensure Their Reproductive Health and Well-Being: It's Their Right and Our Duty: A Field Resource for Programming with and for Refugee Adolescents and Youth.* Geneva: UNHCR, 2002.

———. "Guidelines on International Protection: 'Membership of a Particular Social Group' within the Context of Article 1A(2) of the 1951 Convention and/or Its 1967 Protocol Relating to the Status of Refugees" (May 7, 2002).

———. *Resettlement Handbook: Revised Edition.* Geneva: UNHCR, July 2002.

———. *UNHCR and Refugee Women: Employment.* Geneva: UNHCR, n.d.

UNHCR Evaluation and Policy Analysis Unit, Health and Community Development Section. *Learning for a Future: Refugee Education in Developing Countries.* Geneva: UNHCR, 2002.

UNHCR, Global Consultations on International Protection. "Practical Aspects of Physical and Legal Protection with Regard to Registration." EC/GC/01/6. Available at www.unhcr.ch/prexcom/globalcon.htm (February 19, 2001).

UNHCR, Global Consultations on International Protection. "Report of the Meetings within the Framework of the Standing Committee (Third Track), Report of the Fourth Meeting in the Third Track 22–24 May 2002." A/AC.96/961 (2002).

UNHCR and Save the Children/U.K. *Note for Implementing and Operational Partners on Sexual Violence and Exploitation of Refugee Children in West Africa.* February 2002.

UNHCR, Technical Support Service. *Guinea: An Assessment of the Situation of Liberian Refugee Women and Children.* Geneva: UNHCR, 1990.

UNHCR, WHO, and UNAID. *Guidelines for HIV Interventions in Emergency Settings.* Geneva: September 4, 1995.

UNHCR and Women's Commission for Refugee Women and Children. *Respect Our Rights: Partnership for Equality, Report on the Dialogue with Refugee Women.* Geneva, Switzerland, June 20–22, 2001.

UNICEF Office of the Special Representative in Phnom Penh. *Cambodia: The Situation of Children and Women.* Phnom Penh: UNICEF, 1990.

U.S. Committee for Refugees. *Funding Crisis in Refugee Assistance: Impact on Refugees.* November 20, 2002.

U.S. Office of Refugee Resettlement. *Annual Report to Congress.* 2001.

Vann, Beth. "Gender-Based Violence: Emerging Issues in Programs Serving Displaced Populations." GBV Global Technical Support Project, JSI Research and Training Institute on behalf of the Reproductive Health for Refugees Consortium (September 2002).

Ward, Jeanne. *If Not Now, When? Addressing Gender-Based Violence in Refugee, Internally Displaced and Post-Conflict Settings: A Global Overview.* New York: Refugee Reproductive Health Consortium, 2002.

Weiss-Fagen, Patricia and Arturo Caballero-Barron. *Refugee Participation Case Study: Guatemalans in Campeche and Quintana Roo, Mexico.* Washington, D.C.: Refugee Policy Group, 1987.

Weiss-Fagen, Patricia. "Refugee Women in El Salvador and Guatemala: Challenges and Lessons of Reintegration." For the International Center for Research on Women (April 2000).

Williams, Tessa and Jeff Crisp. "Namibia Together Again." *Refugees* 79 (1989).

Wingo, Gunilla. *Female Attitudes and Social Well-Being: Preparing for Repatriation; A Pilot Study in Two Afghan Refugee Villages in Baluchistan.* Quetta: UNHCR and Radd Barnen/Swedish Save the Children, 1990.

Women's Commission for Refugee Women and Children. *Report of Delegation to Hong Kong, January 5–12, 1990* (New York: International Rescue Committee, 1990).

———. *Untapped Potential: Adolescents Affected by Armed Conflict.* New York: Women's Commission for Refugee Women and Children, January 2000.

———. *Fear and Hope: Displaced Burmese Women in Burma and Thailand.* New York: Women's Commission for Refugee Women and Children, March 2000.

———. *Behind Locked Doors: Abuse of Refugee Women at the Krome Detention Center.* Report of an investigation into abuse of asylum seekers detained by the Immigration and Naturalization Service at the Krome Detention Center (Miami, October 2000).

———. *Out of Sight, Out of Mind: Conflict and Displacement in Burundi.* New York: Women's Commission for Refugee Women and Children. Available at www.womenscommission.org/reports/index.html (October 2000).

———. *Against All Odds: Surviving the War on Adolescents: Promoting the Protection and Capacity of Ugandan and Sudanese Adolescents in Northern Uganda.* New York: Women's Commission for Refugee Women and Children, 2001.

———. *Innocents in Jail: INS Moves Refugee Women from Krome to Turner Guilford Knight Correctional Center, Miami.* Report of investigations into abuses of women asylum seekers detained by the Immigration and Naturalization Service at the TGK Correctional Center (Miami, July 2001).

———. *Refugee and Internally Displaced Women and Children in Serbia and Montenegro*. New York: Women's Commission for Refugee Women and Children, September 2001.

———. *Rights, Reconstruction and Enduring Peace: Afghan Women and Children after the Taliban*. New York: Women's Commission for Refugee Women and Children, December 2001.

———. *If Not Now, When? Addressing Gender-Based Violence in Refugee, Internally Displaced and Post-Conflict Settings. A Global Overview*. New York: Women's Commission for Refugee Women and Children, 2002.

———. *UNHCR Policy on Refugee Women and Guidelines on Their Protection: An Assessment of Ten Years of Implementation*. New York: Women's Commission for Refugee Women and Children, 2002.

———. *Refugees and AIDS: What Should the Humanitarian Community Do?* New York: Women's Commission for Refugee Women and Children, January 2002.

———. *Precious Resources: Participatory Research Study with Adolescents and Youth in Sierra Leone*. New York: Women's Commission for Refugee Women and Children, April–July 2002.

World Food Program. "Workshop: Women Beneficiaries Speak Out." (Mapel, Bahr el Ghazal, Sudan, February 16–18, 2000).

Index

About the Author

Susan Forbes Martin serves as the Director of the Institute for the Study of International Migration in the School of Foreign Service at Georgetown University. Previously, she served as the Executive Director of the U.S. Commission on Immigration Reform, a bipartisan panel appointed by the president and congressional leadership, and Director of Research and Programs at the Refugee Policy Group. She served as Managing Editor of *World Migration Report: 2000* and is the author of numerous monographs and articles on immigration and refugee policy. Dr. Martin is also a founder and member of the Board of the Women's Commission for Refugee Women and Children.